Dear Parents

When using this workbook, it is important to read the instructions aloud and answer any questions your child may have, offering help and plenty of encouragement along the way. This will help develop new language and thinking skills, and consequently build self confidence in your child.

The emphasis is on interactive cooperation between parent and child, with guidance on which questions to ask.
It's important not to work in the workbook for more than 5 minutes at the time, so do a little each time to keep it fun.
I hope you and your child have an enjoyable experience using this workbook.

Developed by: Nitza Rozenblum
Author: Nitza Rozenblum
Layout, illustrations and graphic design: Inna Davidovich
Linguistics Editor: Michelle Woolf
No part of this publication may be reproduced, copied, photocopied photographed, translated, stored on a retrieval system, broadcast or recorded in any electronic, optical or mechanical manner. Any form of usage of the material included in this workbook is strictly forbidden, unless explicit permission is granted by the author.

All Rights Reserved by Nitza Rozenblum (2017)

pages	Subject	Description
3,20,38,56,74	Numbers 1,2,3,4,5 Counting And Cardinality.	Recognizing numbers - counting and writing.
4,21,39,57,75	Compare Quantities	The ability to compare groups by counting.
5,22,40,58,76	Fine Motor Skills	Training in pencil control.
6,23,41,59,77	Make Sets	
7,24,42,53,60,78	Matching	Finding the correct object.
8,25,43,61,79,90	Patterns	The ability to identify, and create repetitive patterns.
9,26,44,62,80	Tall And Short Wide & Narrow	Knowledge of concepts.
10,27,45,63,81	Size Relations	Matching according to size: small, medium and big
11,50,84	The Exception	Finding the odd one out.
12, 16, 29,33,46,52,64,67,82,85	Matching Numbers To Quantities	Circling the correct quantity.
13,18,30,36,47,54,65,72,83,89	Matching Quantities	Matching according to the quantity
14,31,48	The Missing object.	The ability to find the missing object in a series of objects.
28	Pairs	Familiarity with the concept of a pair by connecting pairs of animals.
17,19,34,53,68,71,86	Geometry	Recognizing triangles, squares and circles.
19,37,55,73	Complete	
35,51,66,70,71,92	Following The Instructions	
88	Compare Quantities	The ability to compare groups by counting.
91	Challenge	

One
Circle and color 1 of each:

Write the number 1 using the arrows as a guide:

One
Circle sets of one in each row:

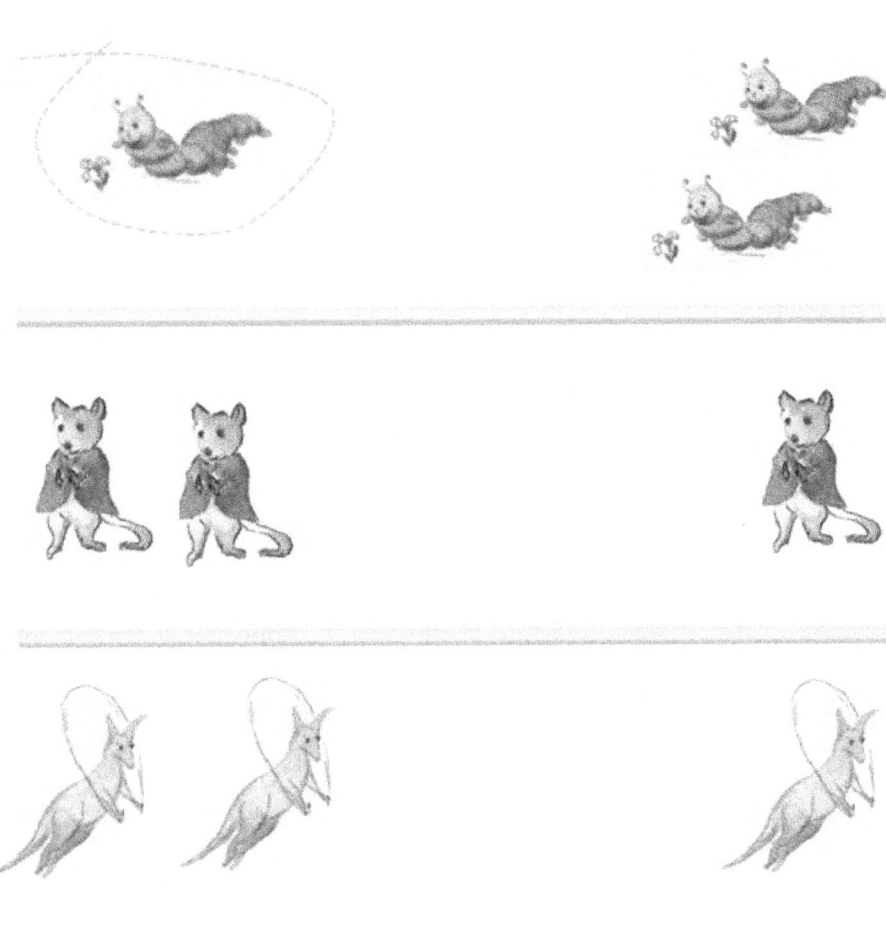

Join each rabbit to its carrot:
(start at the black dot)

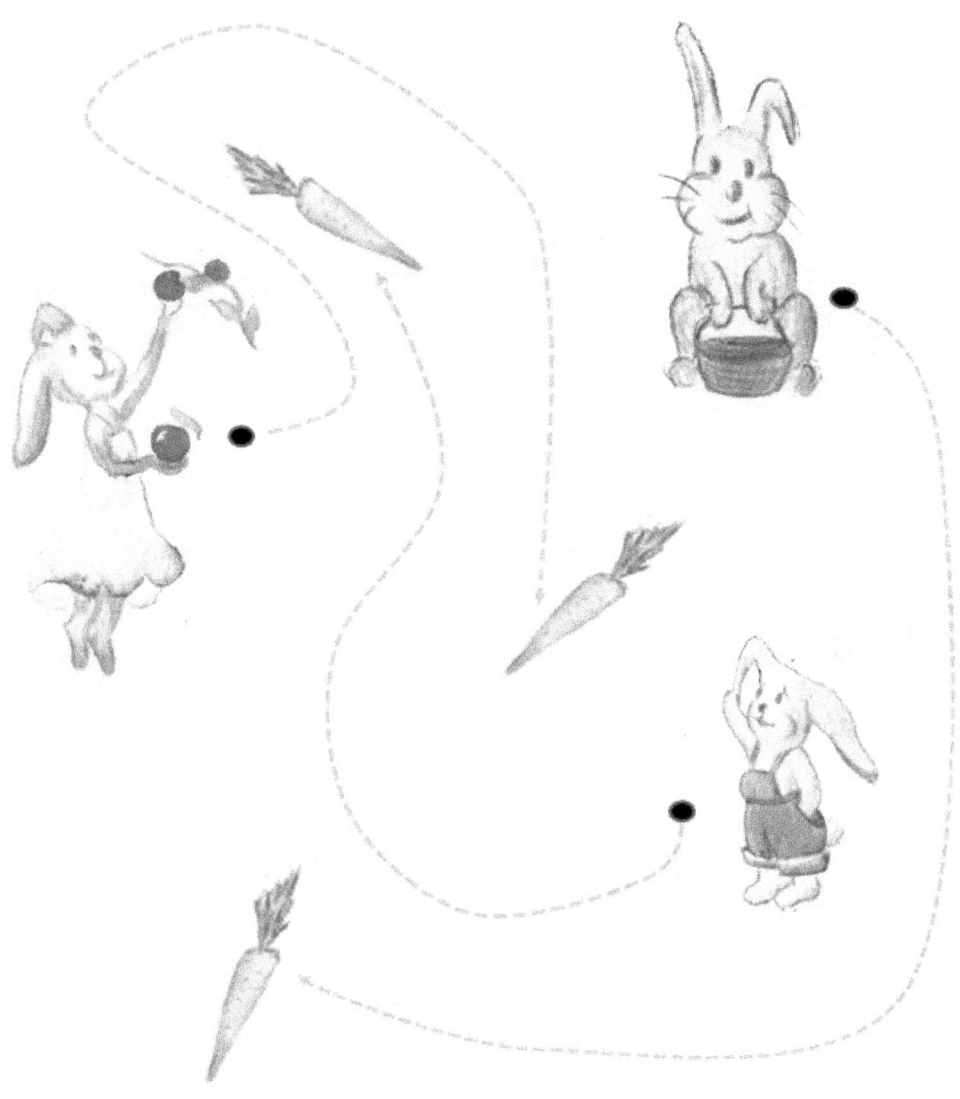

Ask your child to use his finger to trace over the line, before using a pencil.

Make Sets
Circle 1 corncob for each basket:

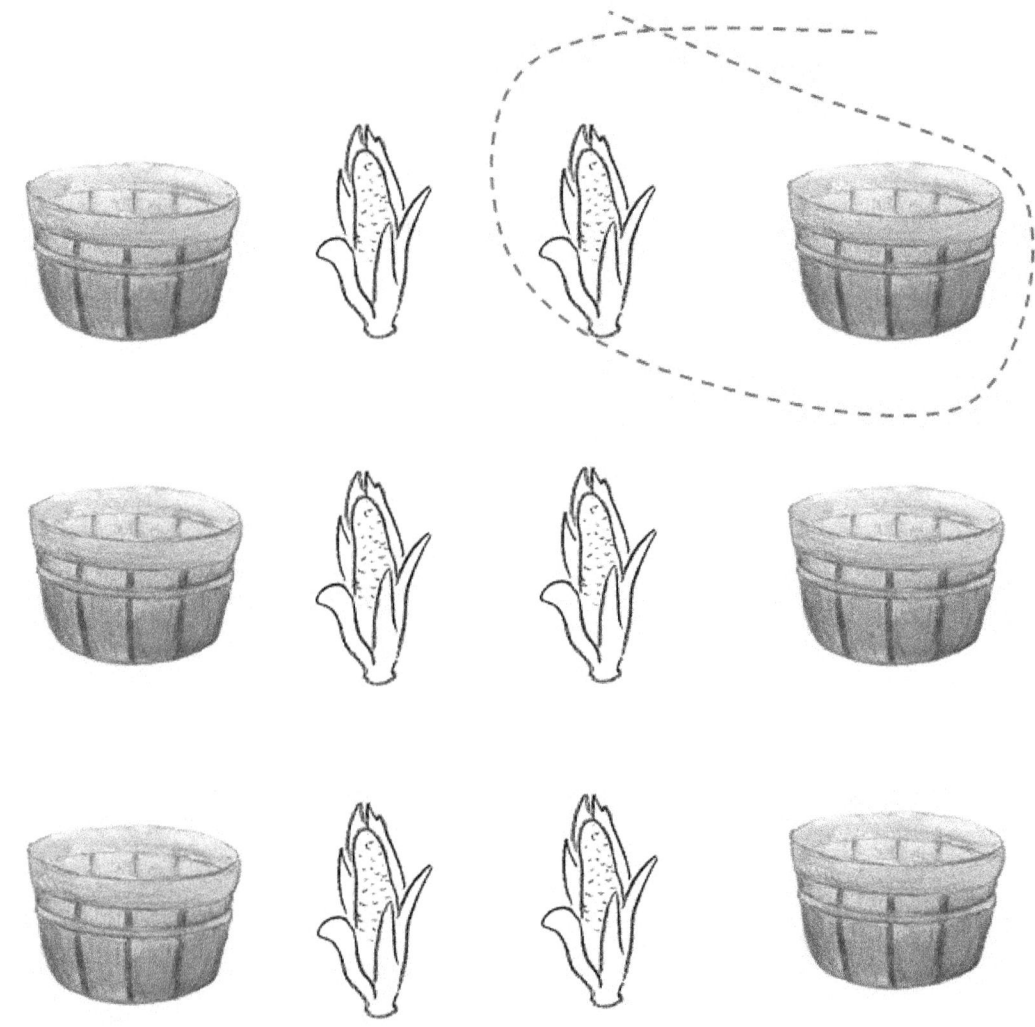

Question: Are there more baskets or more corncobs?

Matching
Color the matching one:

Recognizing Patterns

Color the dots according to the pattern, encouraging your child to name the colors. Follow the instructions.

Red, yellow, red, yellow...

◯ ◯ ◯ ◯ ◯ ◯

Blue, green, blue, green ...

◯ ◯ ◯ ◯ ◯ ◯

Yellow, blue, yellow, ...

◯ ◯ ◯ ◯ ◯ ◯

Write the number 1 using the arrows as a guide:

Tall & Short
Circle the taller animal in each row:

Small Medium Big

In each row, draw the missing object according to its size:

Small apple

Circle The Odd One Out:

How Many?

In each row, count and circle the correct number:

Write the number 1 using the arrows as a guide:

Color the set with the bigger amount in each row:

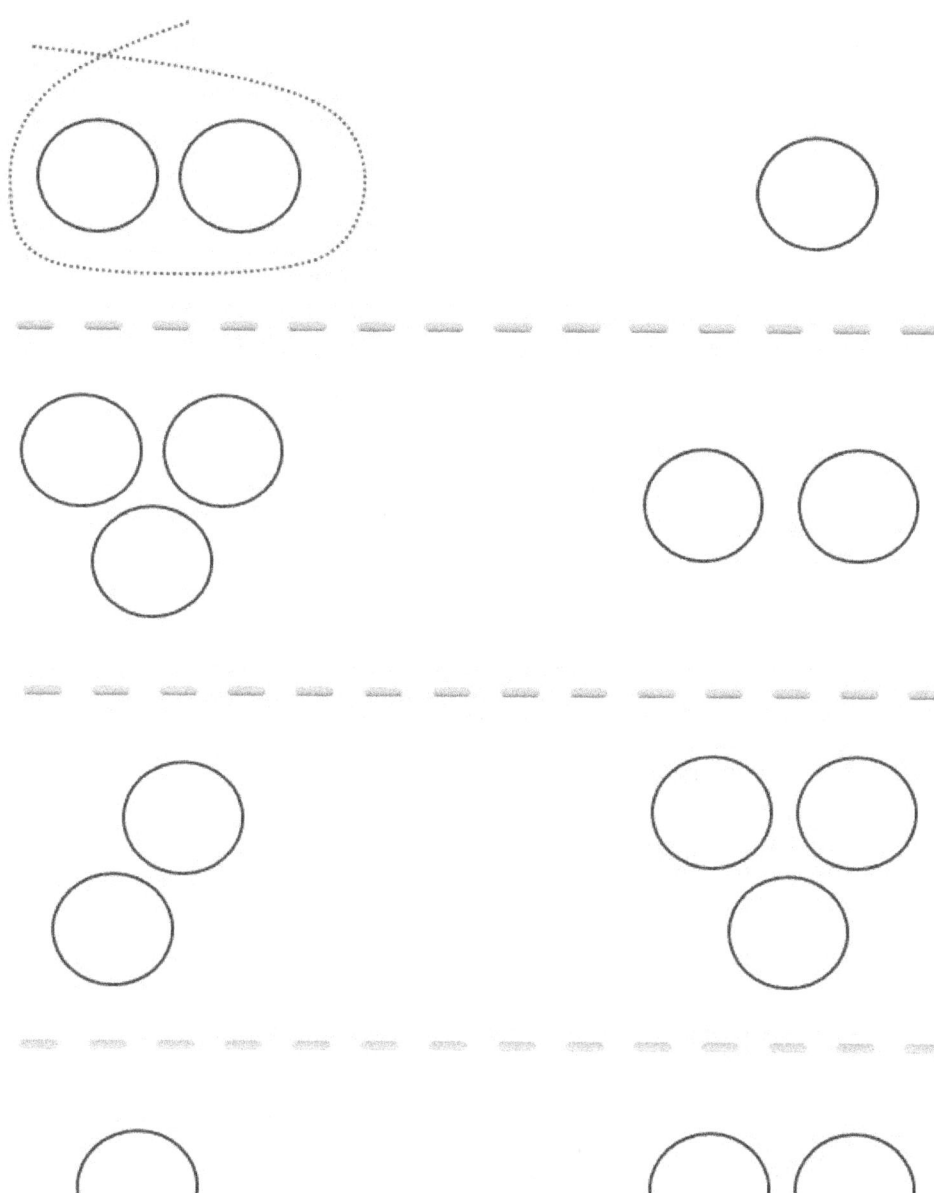

Fill in the missing one:

(Also possible to draw)

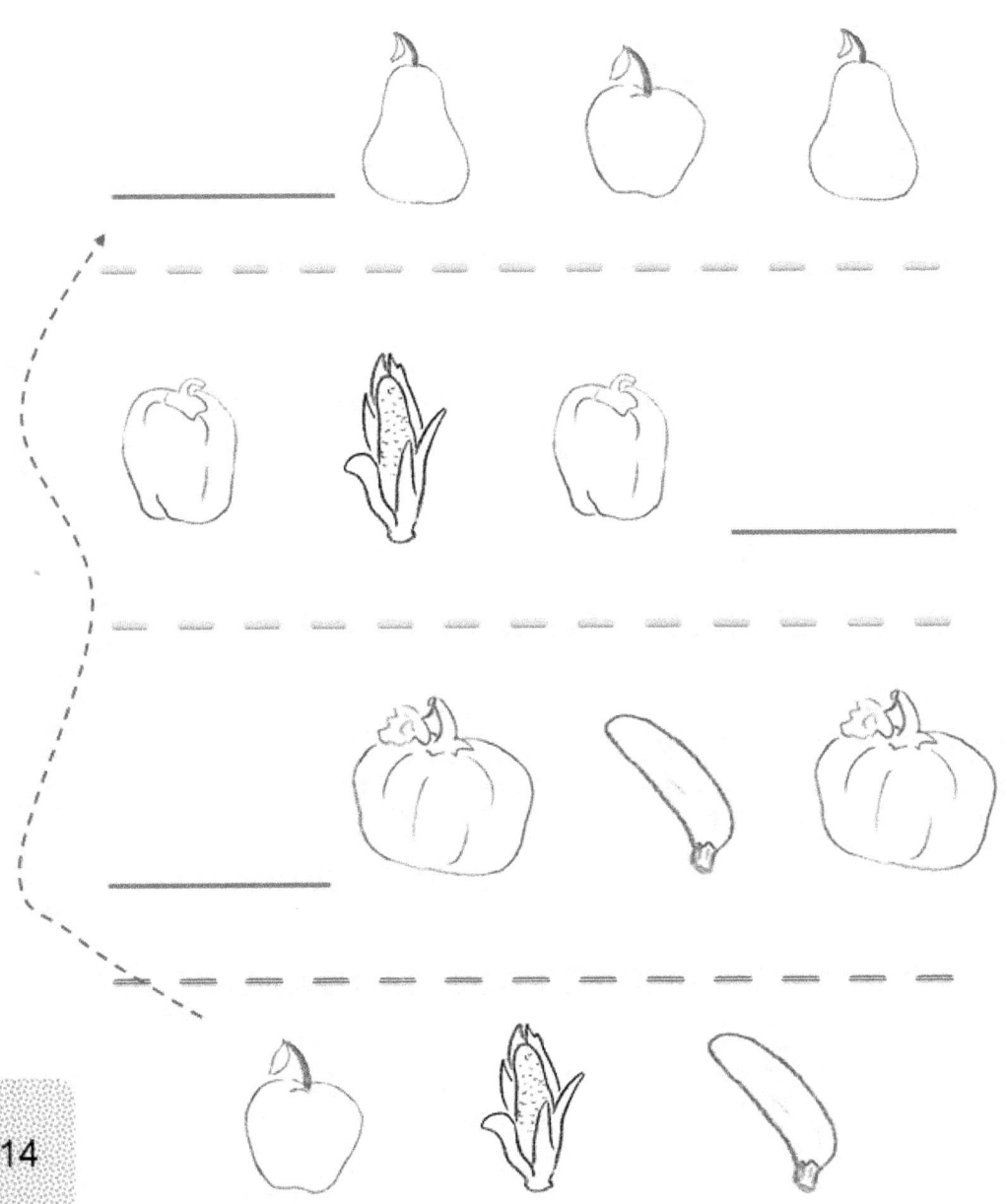

Join Pairs

Matching Numbers To Quantities

Draw a line matching the number to its amount:

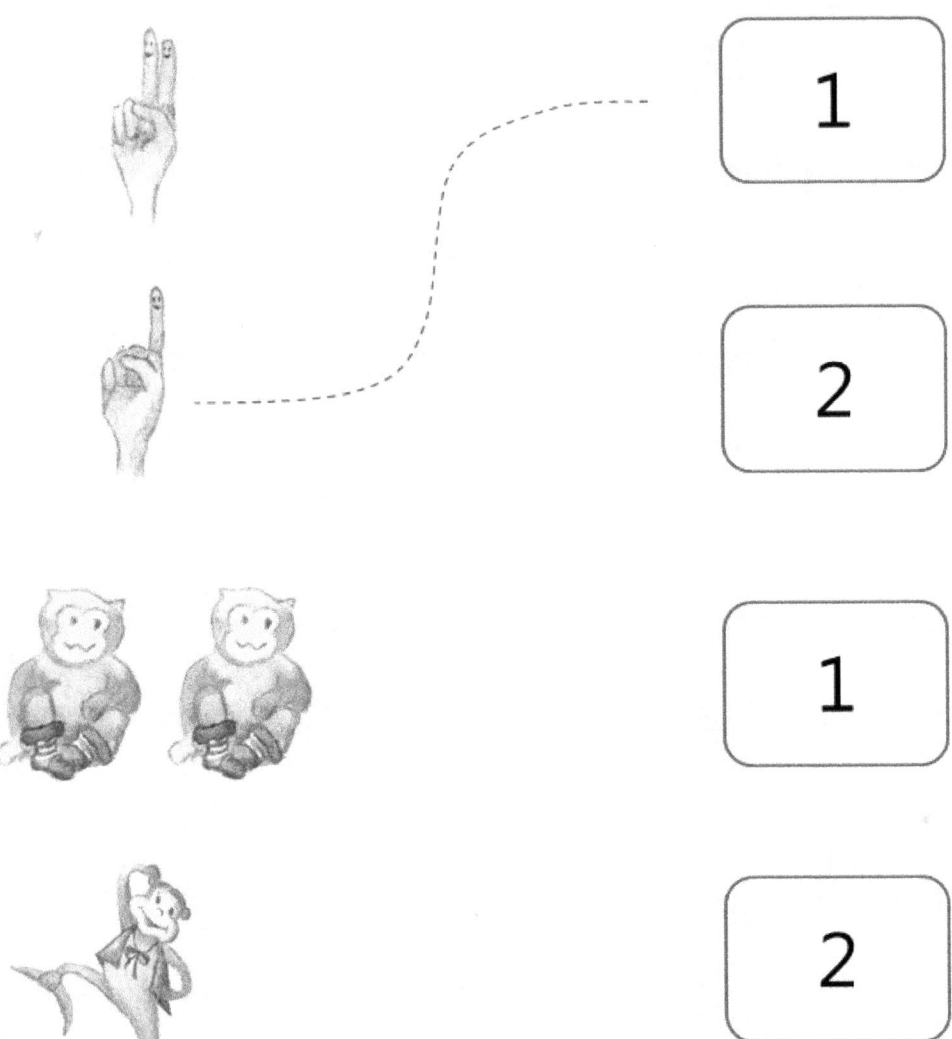

Let's draw squares

Join the dots, starting at the black dot, using the arrows as a guide.

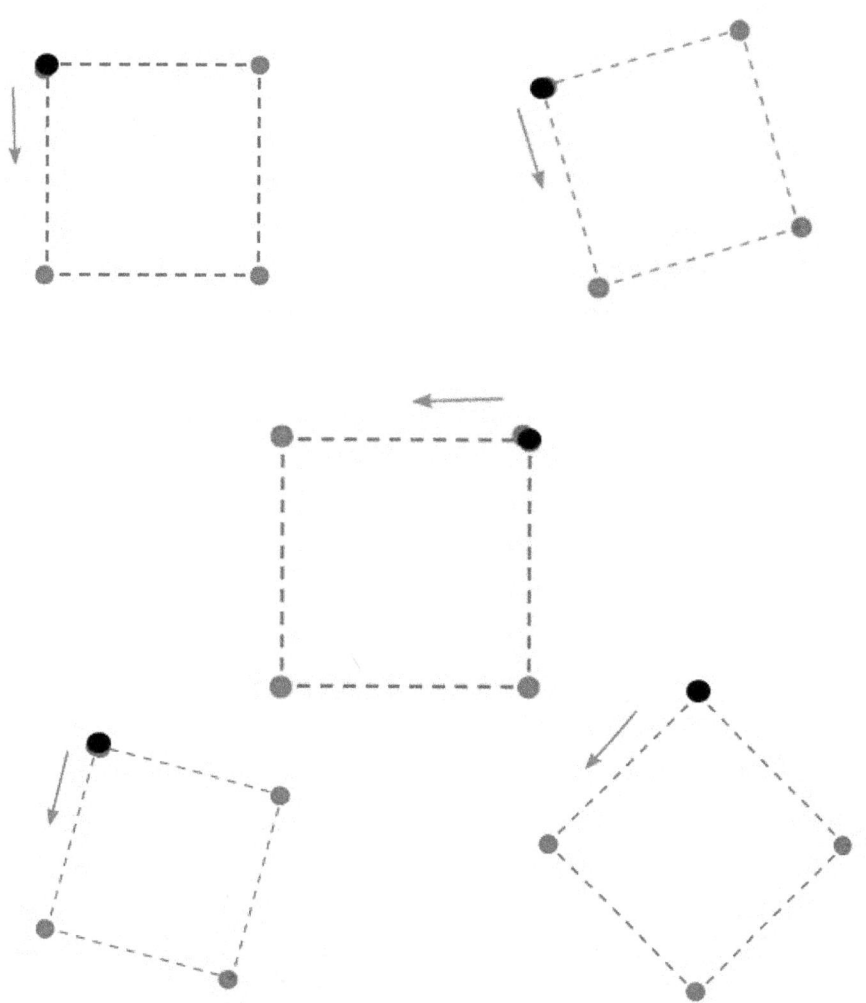

Circle the set with the Smaller amount in each row:

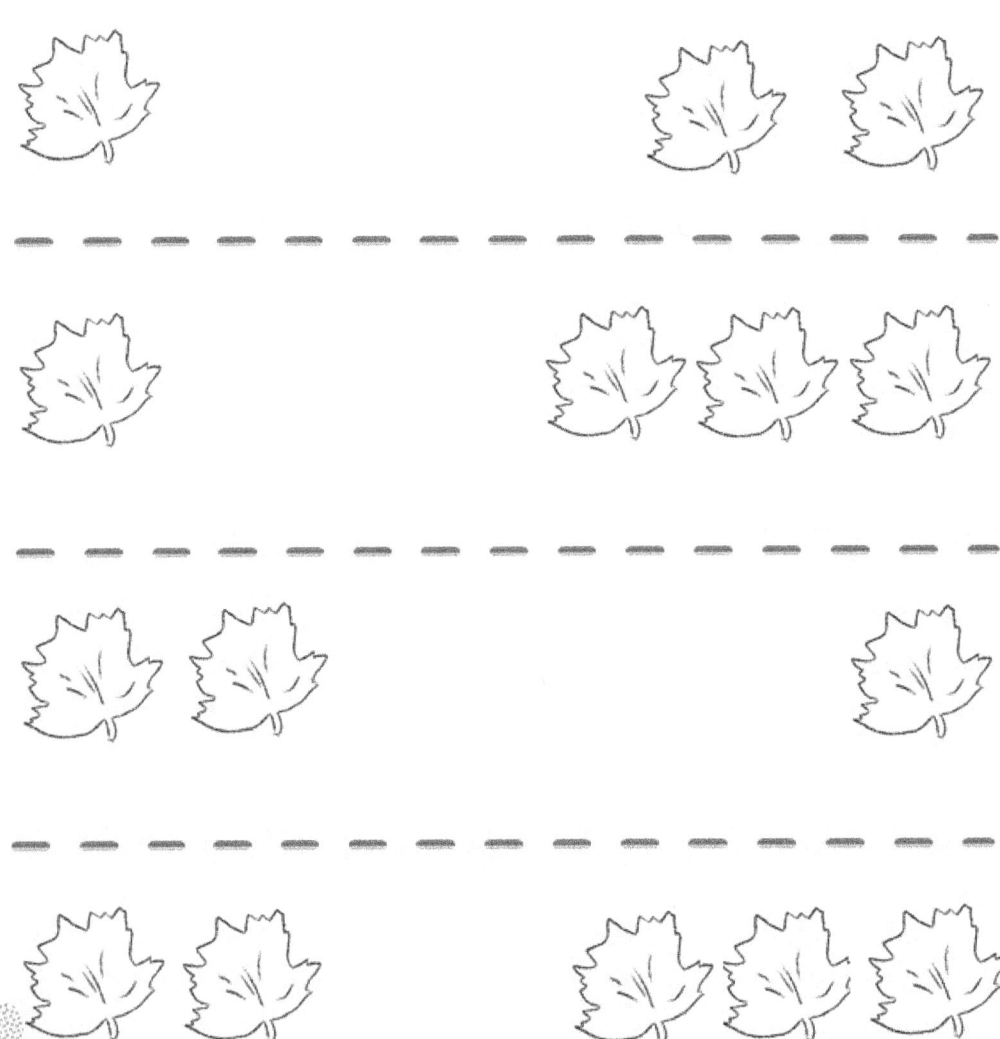

Complete:

Cut out and paste the matching cards, from the page at the end of the workbook.

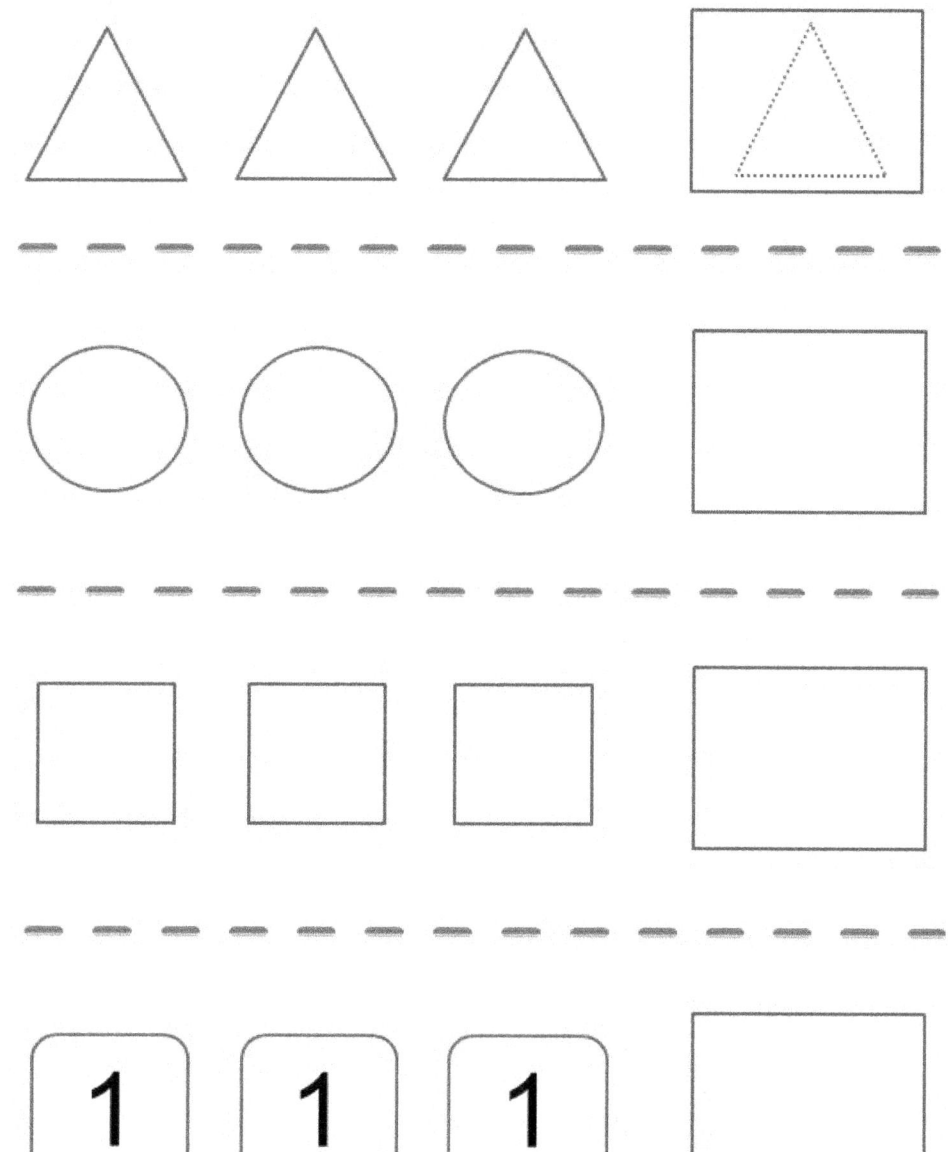

Two
Circle and color 2 of each:

Write the number 2 using the arrows as a guide:

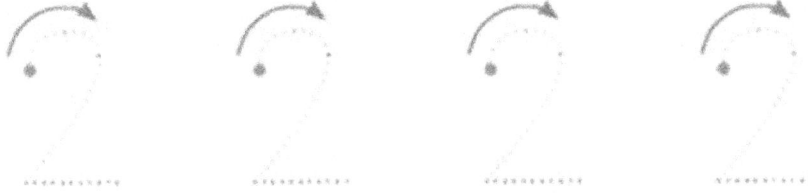

Two
Circle sets of 2 in each row:

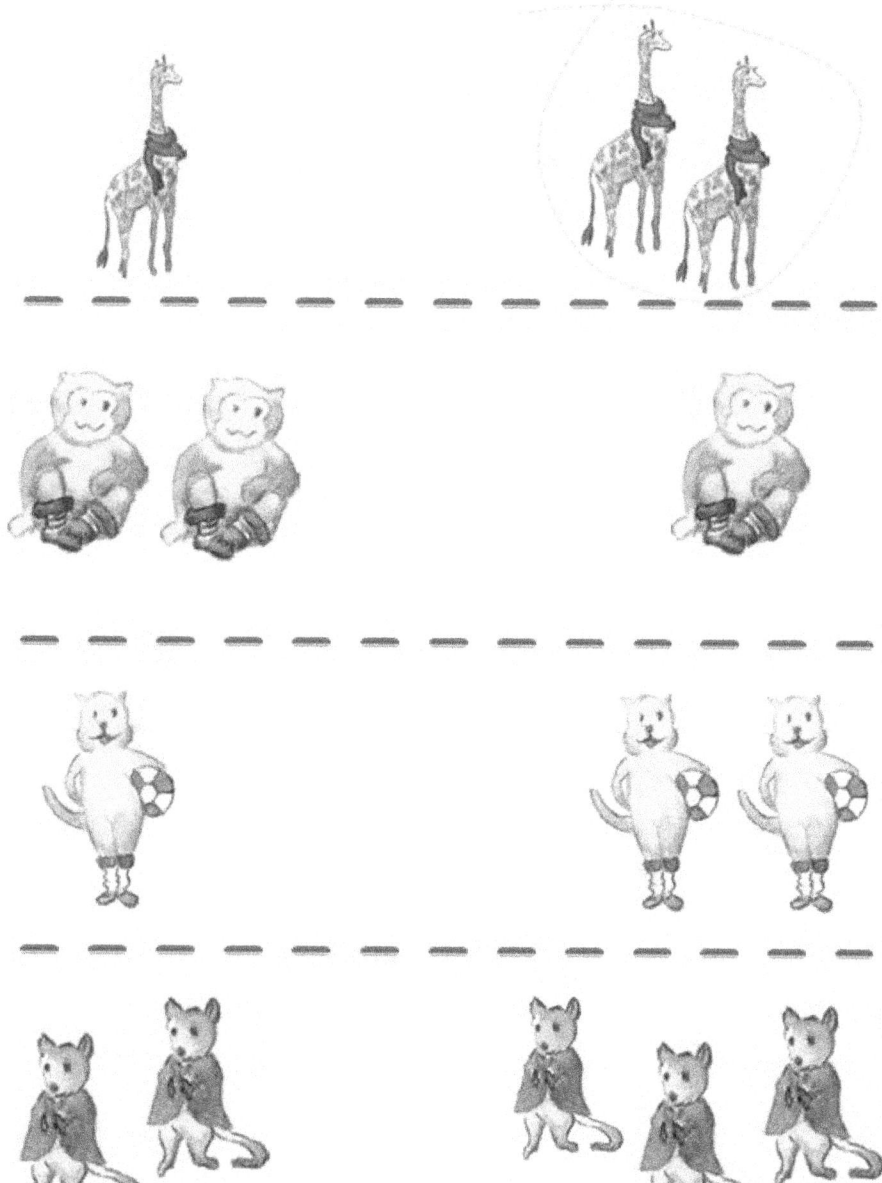

Join each panda to its bamboo branch:

(start at the black dot)

Ask your child to use his finger to trace over the line, before using a pencil.

Make Sets

Circle and color 2 apples for each bowl:

(Color the apples different colors for each bowl)

Question: Are there more bowls or more apples?
(It's possible to draw another bowl for the remaining apples).

Matching

Color the matching one:

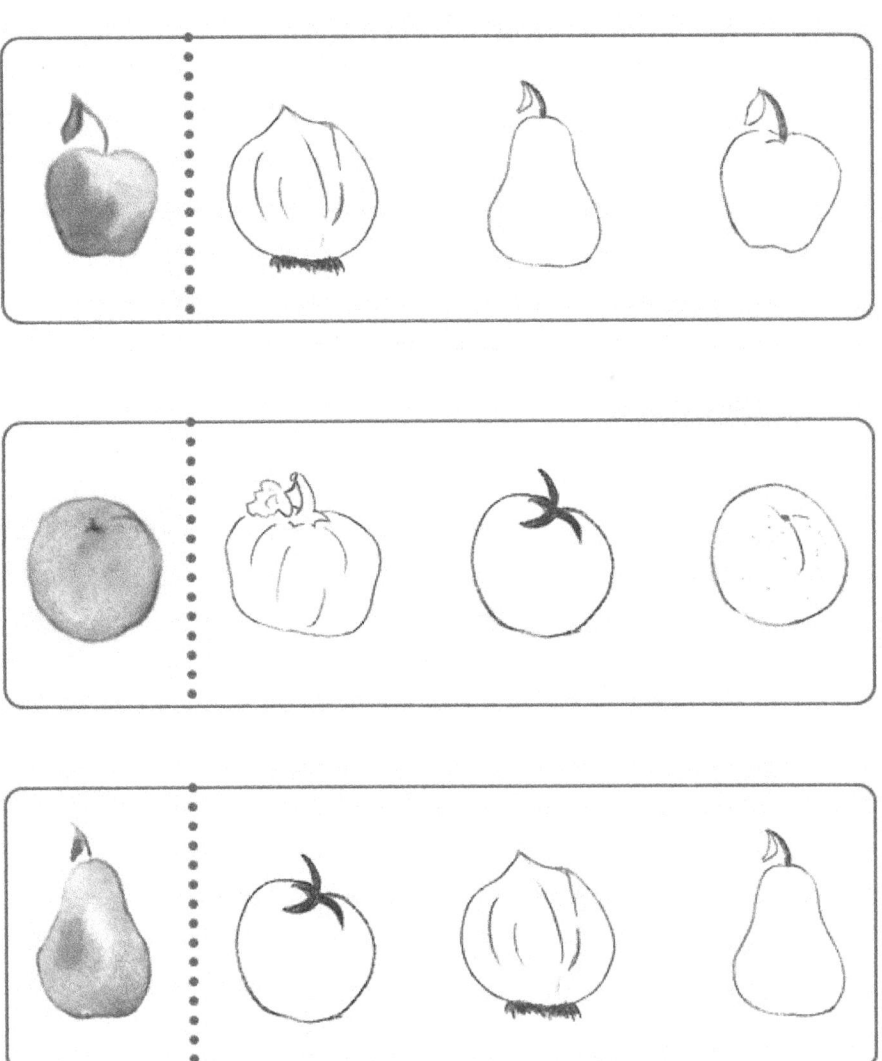

Recognizing Patterns

Color the dots according to the pattern, encouraging your child to name the colors.

Green, orange, green, ...

○ ○ ○ ○ ○

Blue, pink, blue, ...

○ ○ ○ ○ ○

Yellow, brown, yellow, ...

○ ○ ○ ○ ○

Write the number 2 using the arrows as a guide:

2 2 2 2

Wide & Narrow
Circle the wide object in each row:

 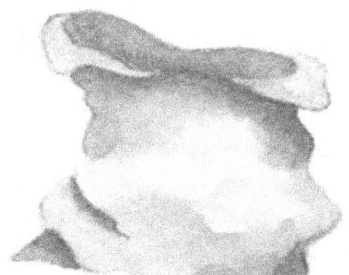

Small Medium Big

In each row, draw the missing object according to its size:

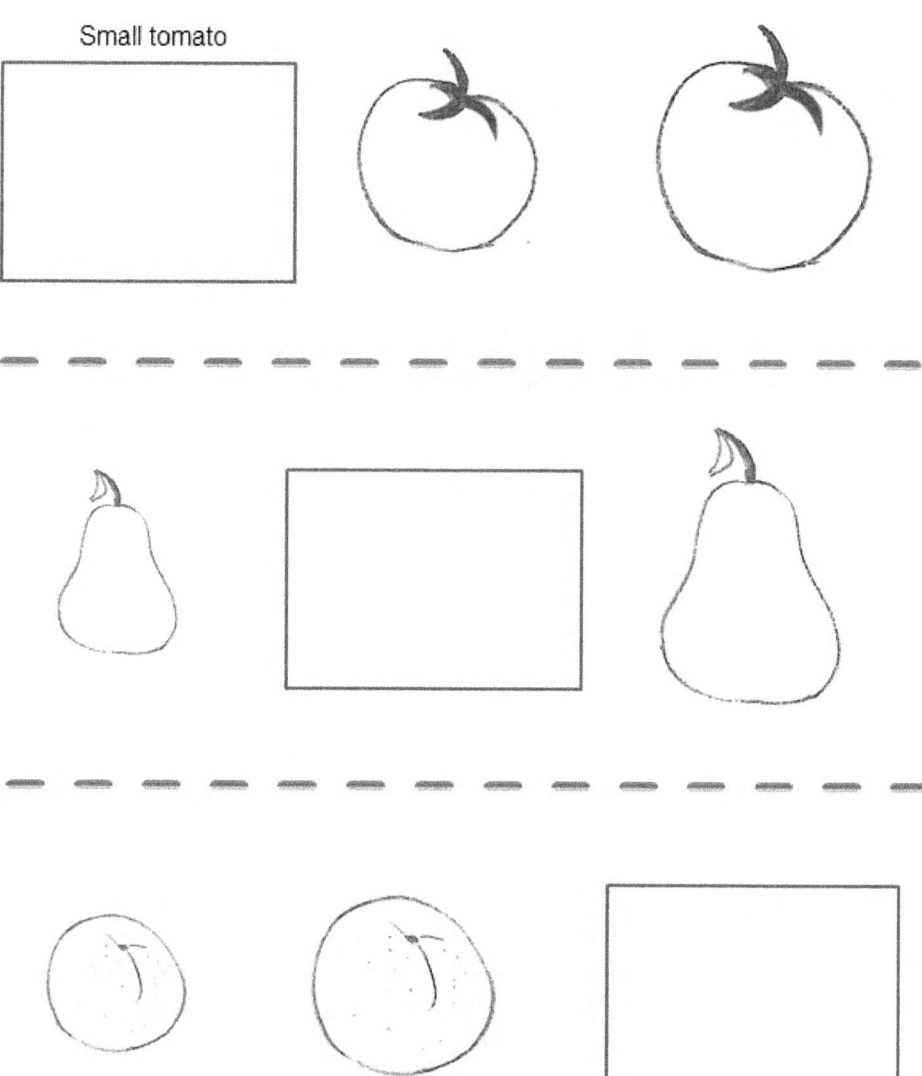

Small tomato

Join pairs

How many?

In each row, count and circle the correct number:

Write the number 2 using the arrows as a guide:

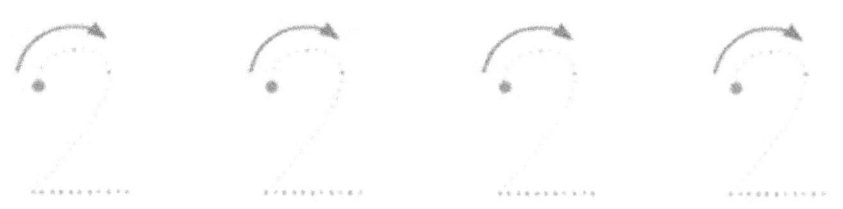

Color the set with the Bigger amount in each row:

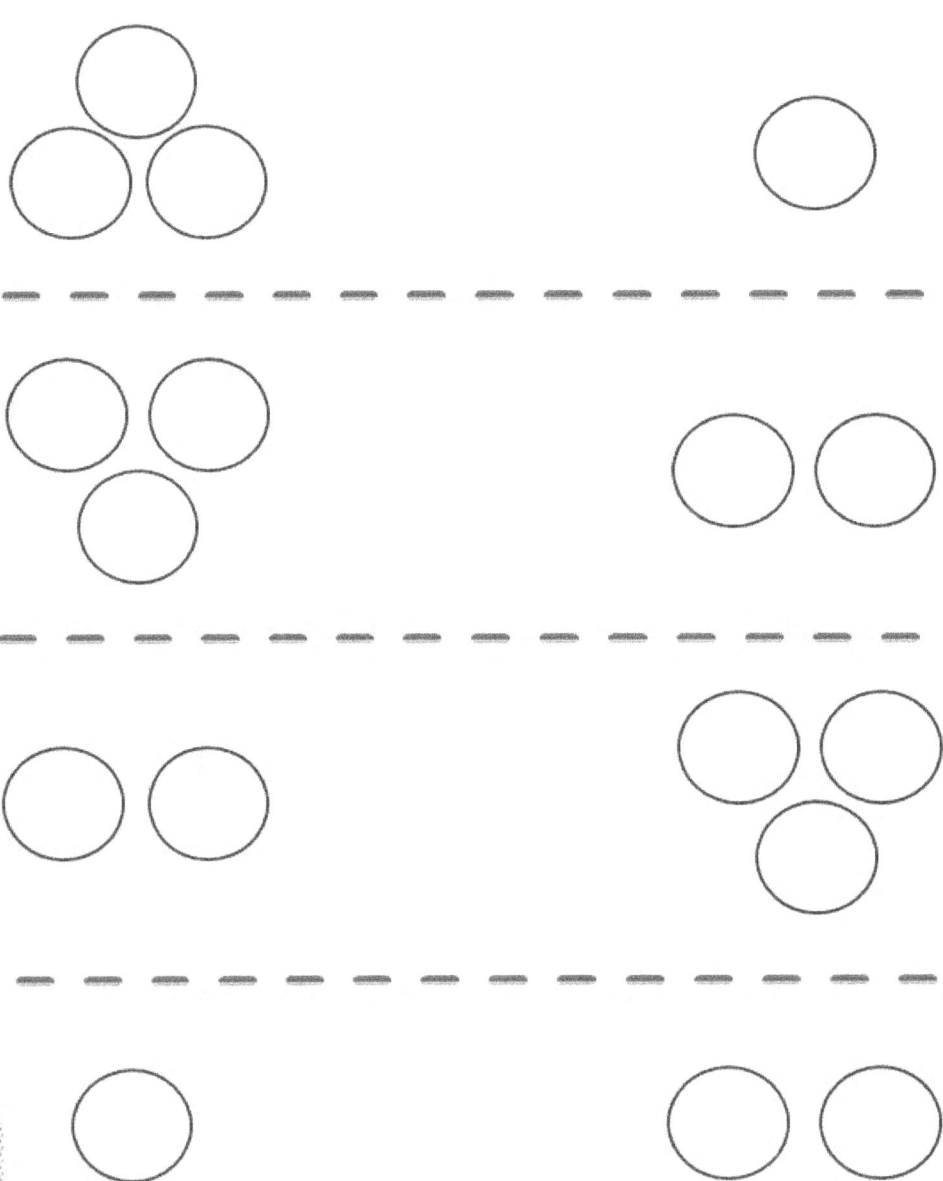

Fill in the missing one:
(Also possible to draw)

How Many Squares?

Color the squares in each column and write the amount.

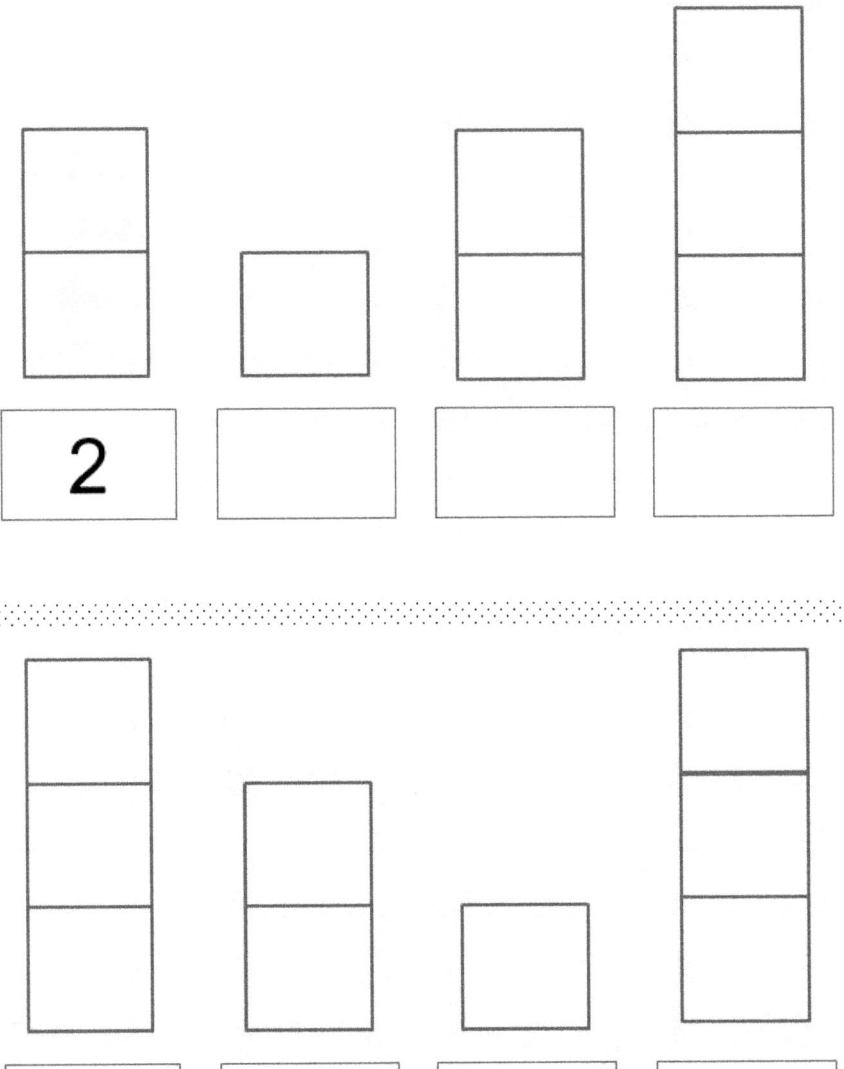

Draw a line matching the number to its amount:

     1

   2

   3

Let's draw triangles

Join the dots, starting at the black dot, using the arrows as a guide.

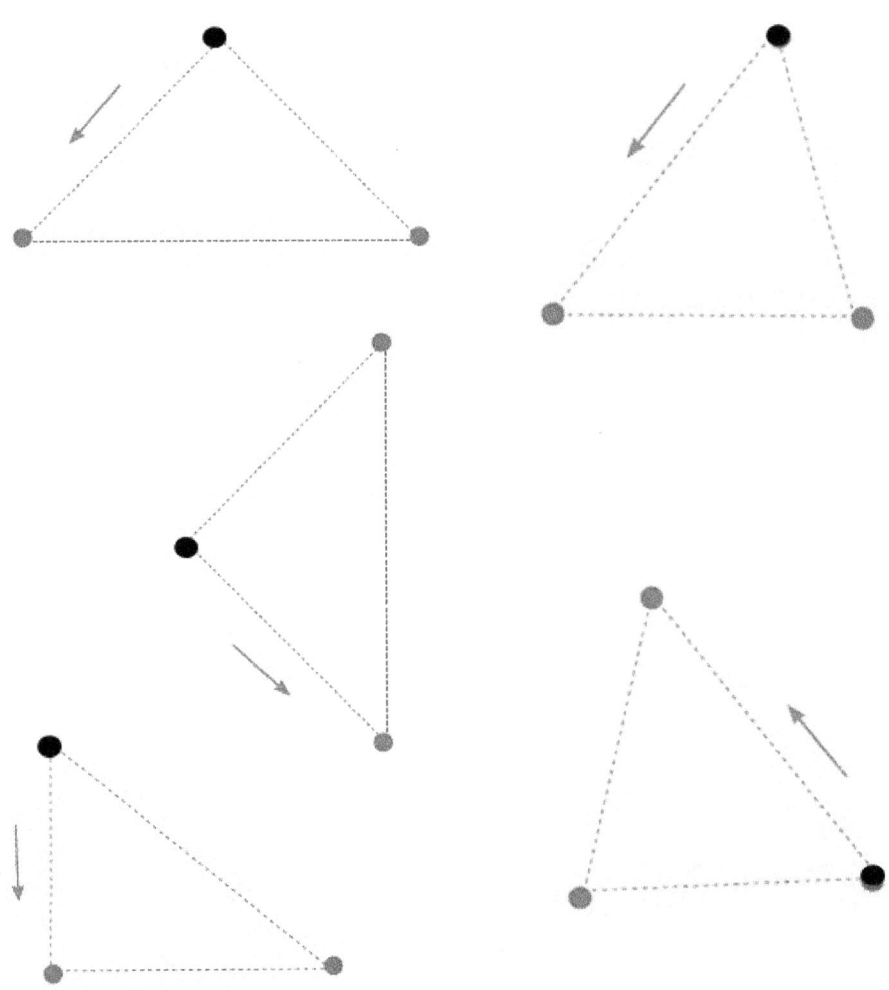

Follow the instructions:

Draw 1 leaf for each turtle.

Draw 2 bananas for each monkey.

Draw 3 bones for each dog.

Color the set with the Smaller amount in each row:

- -

- -

Complete:

Cut out and paste the matching cards, from the page at the end of the workbook.

Three
Circle and color 3 of each:

Write the number 3 using the arrows as a guide:

Three
Circle sets of 3 in each row:

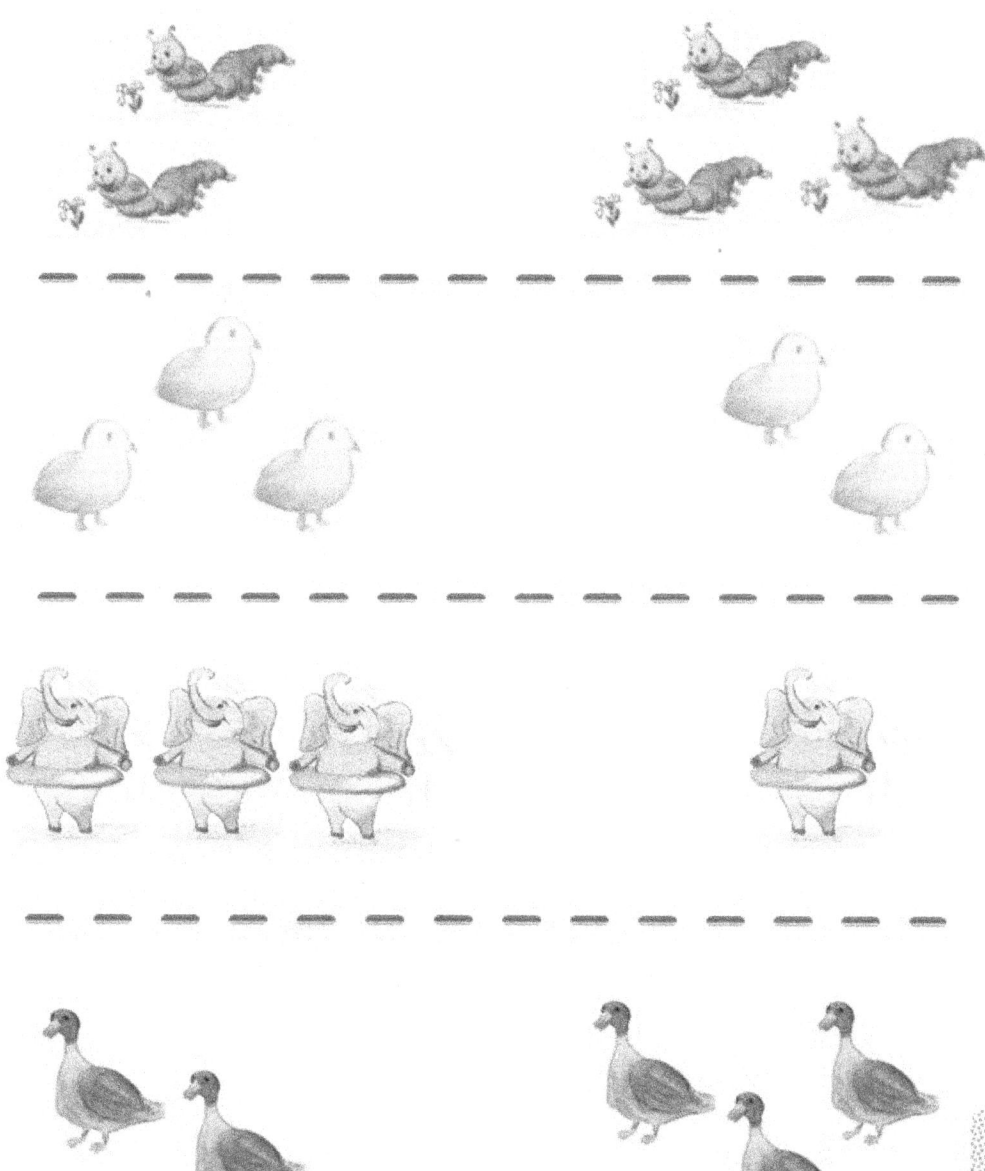

Join each chicken to its egg:
(start at the black dot)

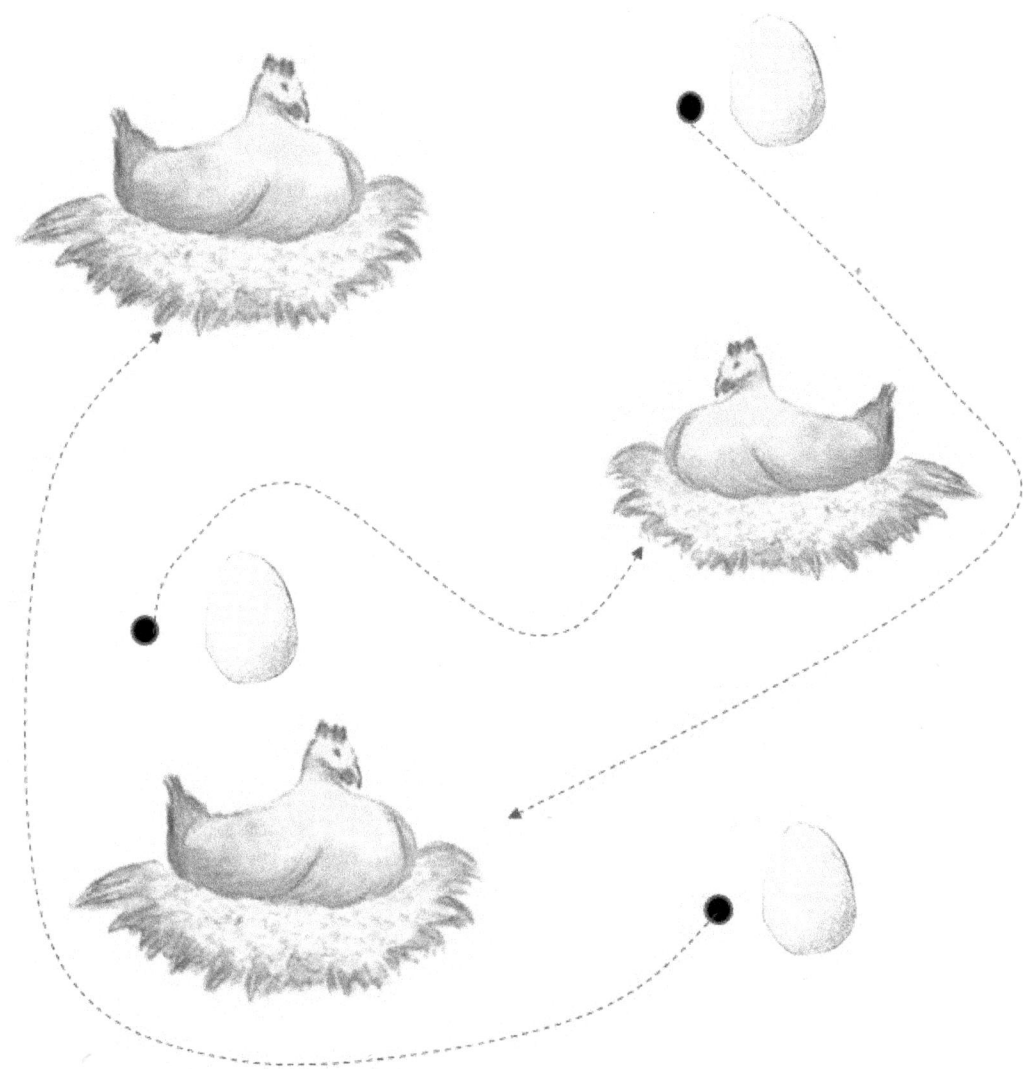

Ask your child to use his finger to trace over the line, before using a pencil.

Make Sets

Circle and color 3 bees for each beehive:

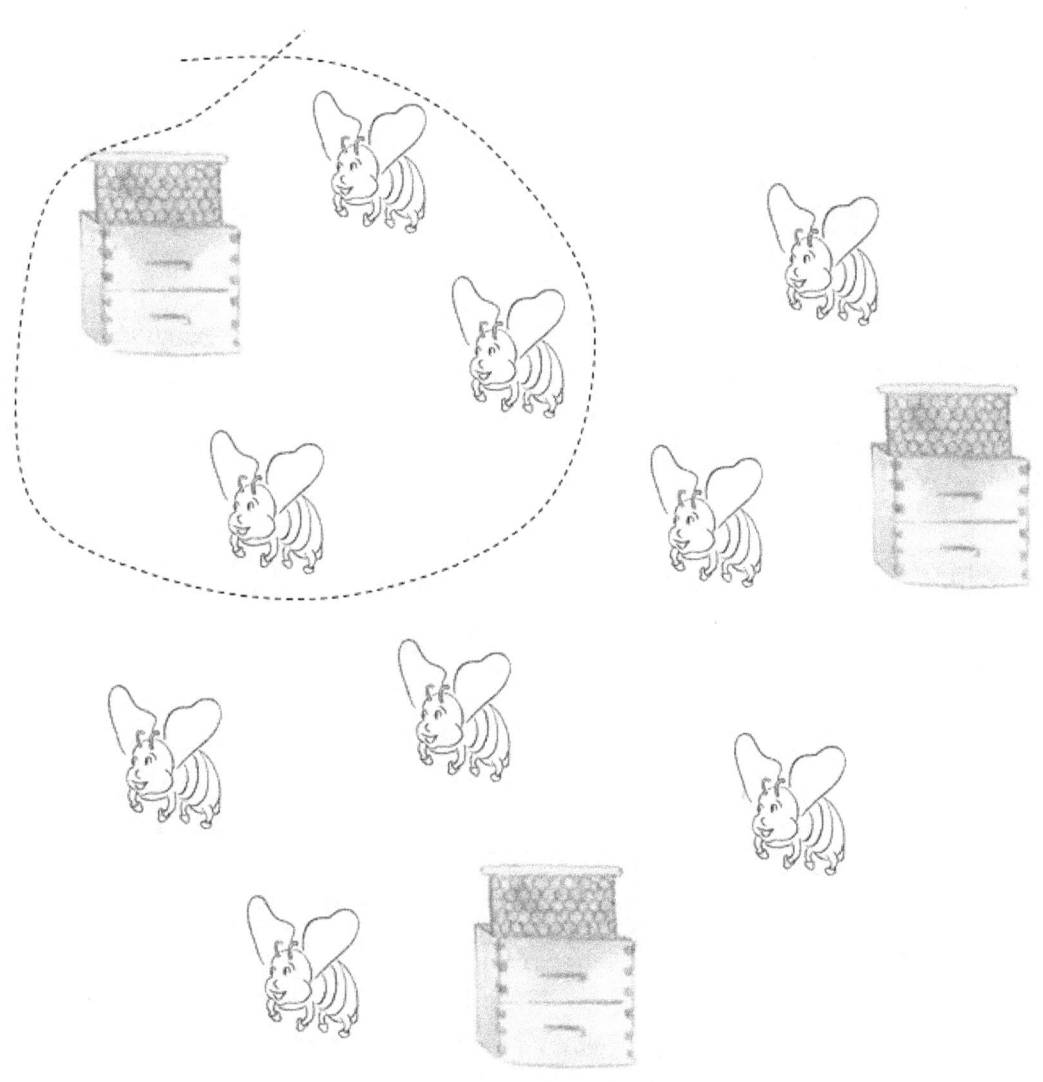

Question: Are there more beehives or more bees?
Question: How many bees are there without beehive?

Matching
Color the matching one:

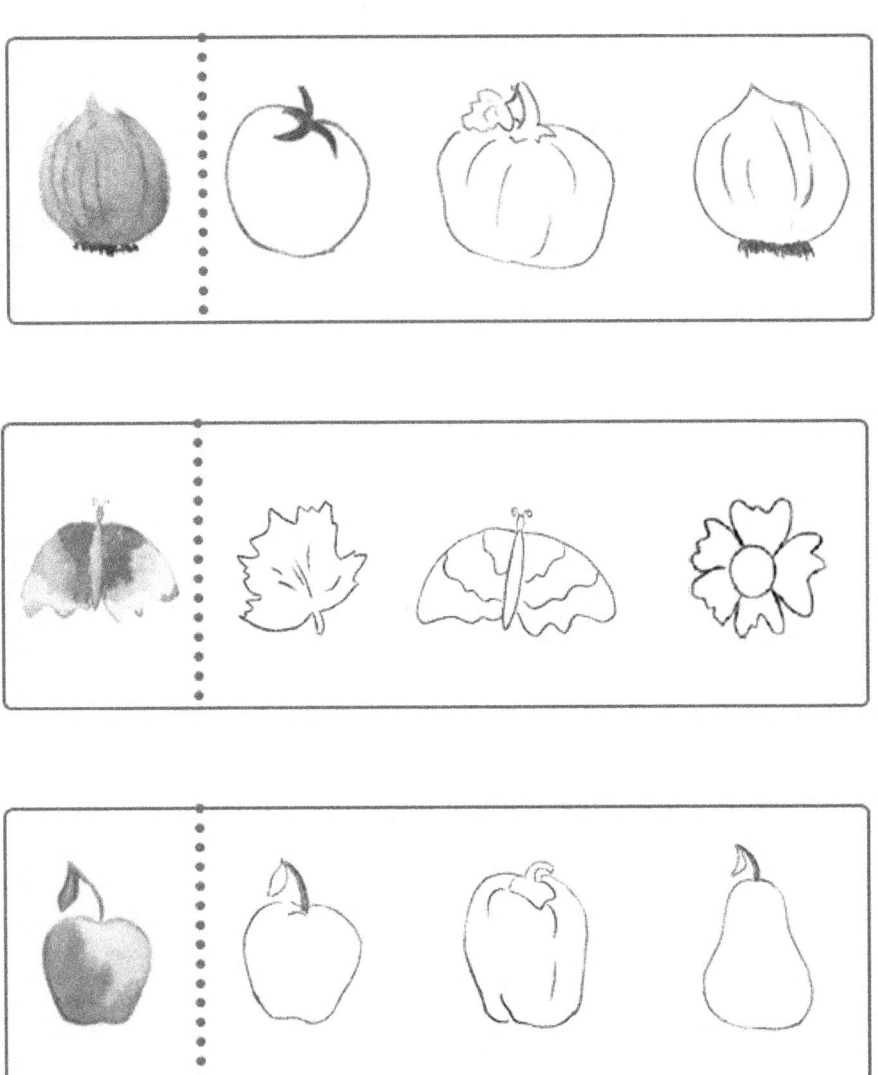

Recognizing Patterns

Color the dots according to the pattern, encouraging your child to name the colors.

Red, green, red green ...

○ ○ ○ ○ ○ ○ ○

Green, yellow, green, yellow...

○ ○ ○ ○ ○ ○ ○

Blue, pink, blue, pink ...

○ ○ ○ ○ ○ ○ ○

Write the number 3 using the arrows as a guide:

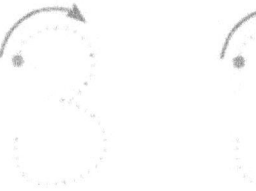  

Tall & Short
Circle the taller one in each set:

Small Medium Big

In each row, draw the missing animal according to its size:

How Many?

In each row, count and circle the correct number:

Write the number 3 using the arrows as a guide:

Color the set with the Bigger amount in each row:

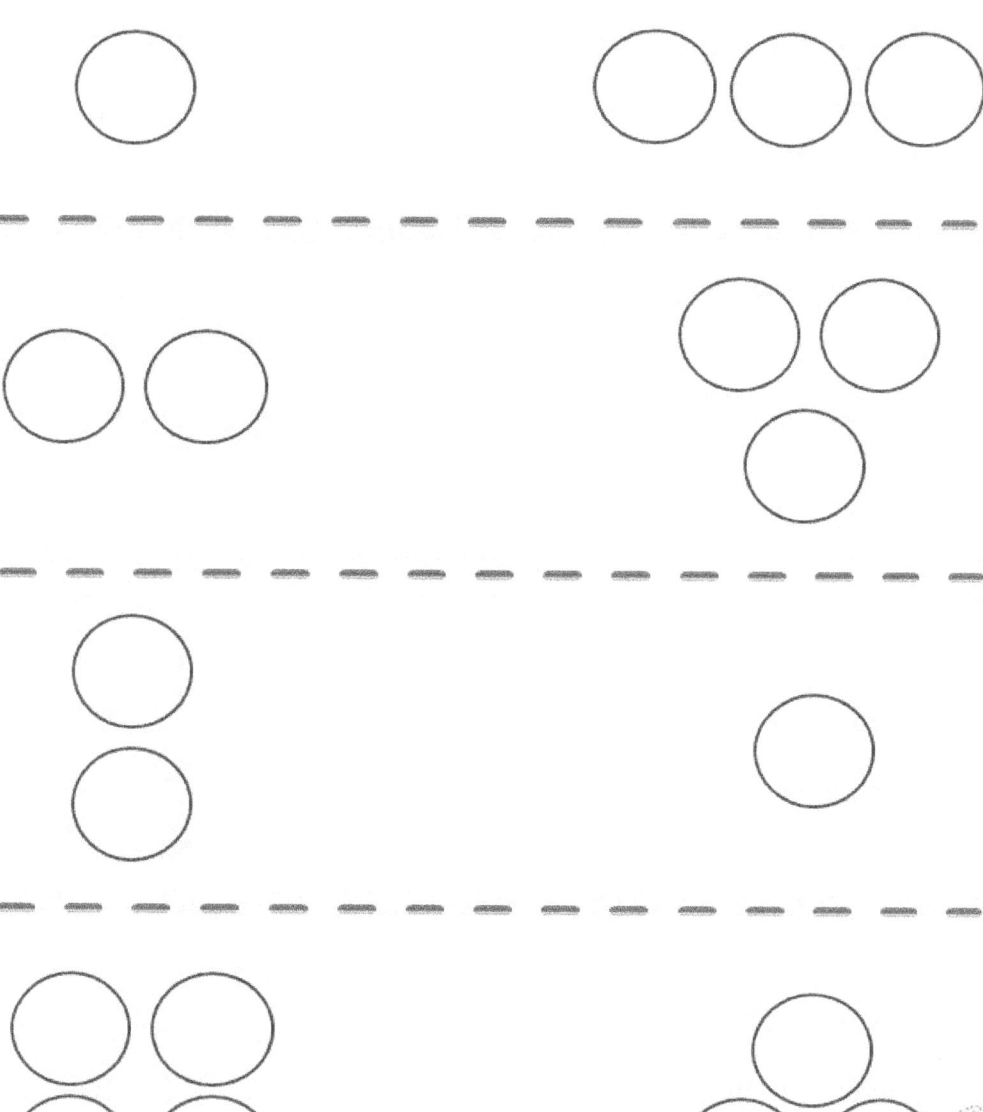

The Missing Animal

Draw a line from an animal at the bottom on the page, to its correct place.

  _____

_____

 _____

Color squares according to the number.

3

2

1

5

4

Circle the Odd One Out:

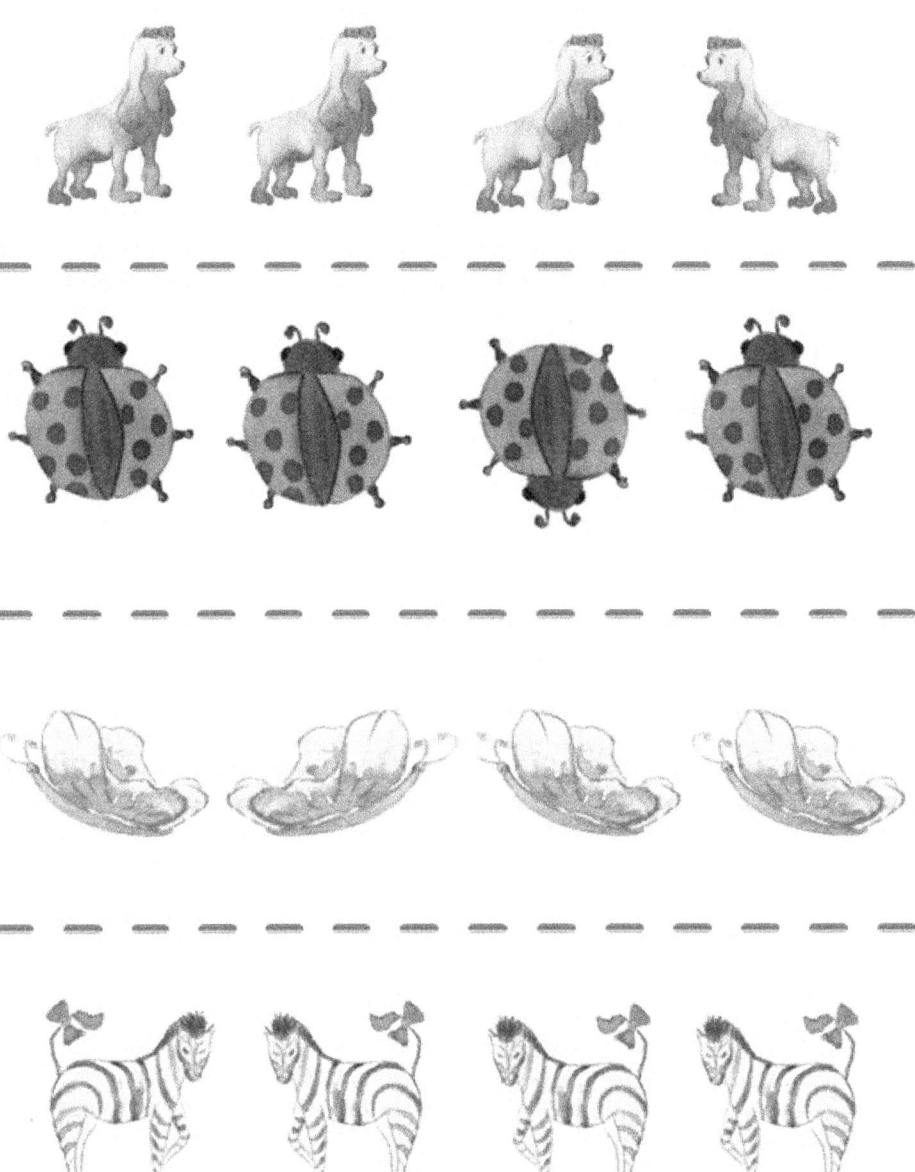

Follow the instructions:

Color the flowers pink.

Color the leaves yellow.

Color the mushrooms brown.

Matching Numbers To Quantities

Draw a line matching the number to its amount:

Matching

Color the matching shape:

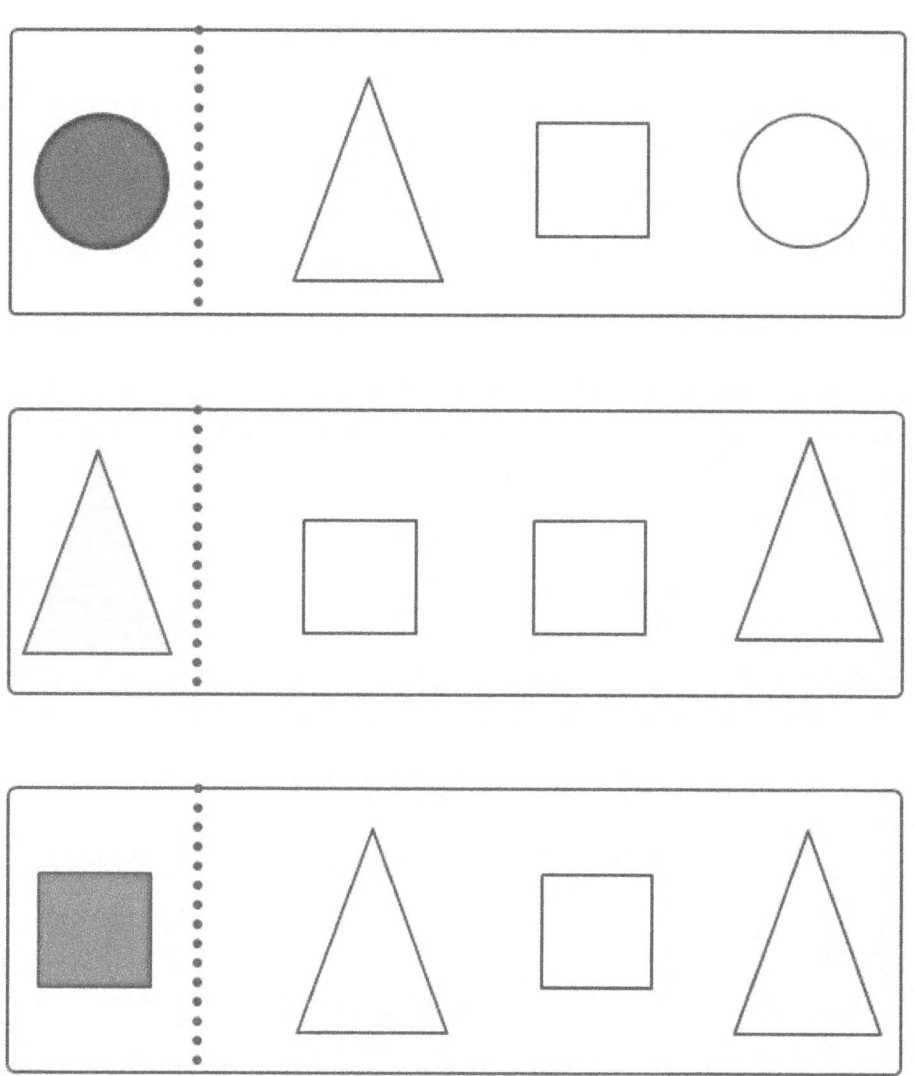

Color the set with the Smaller amount in each row:

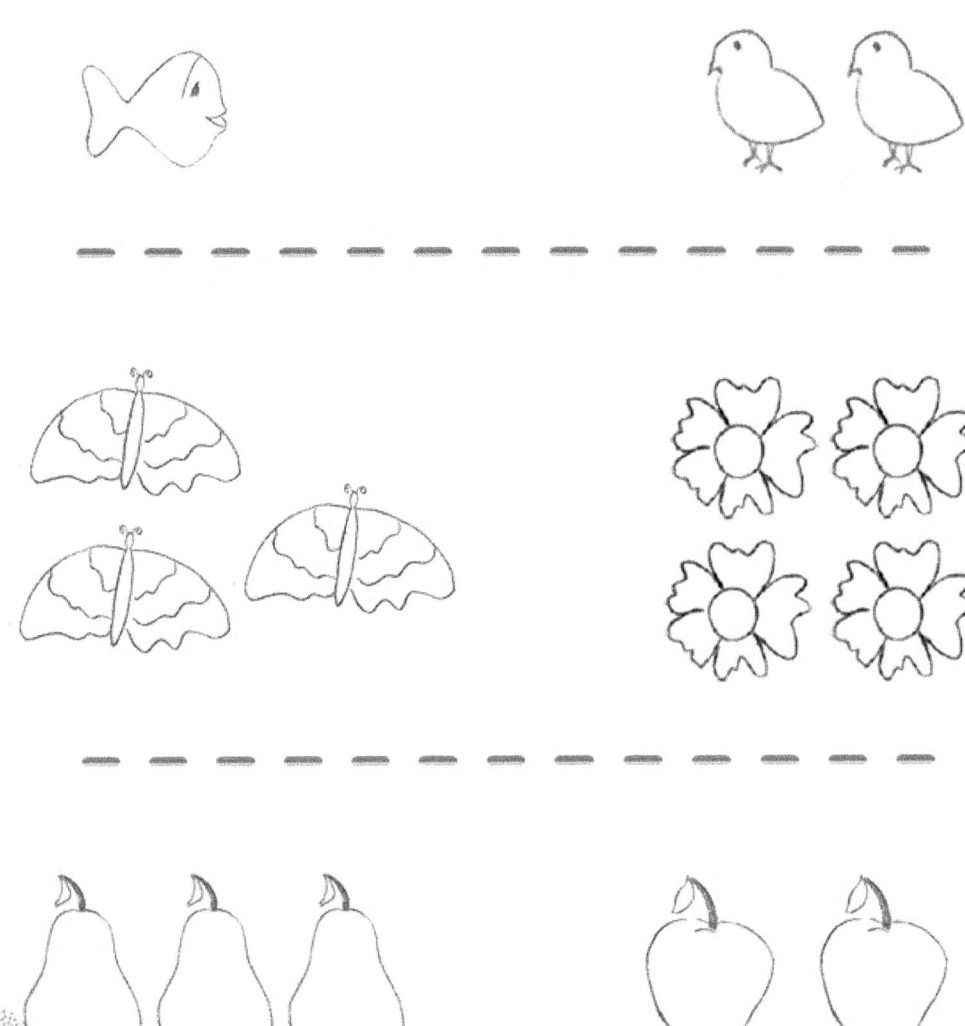

Complete:

Cut out and paste the matching cards, from the page at the end of the workbook.

Four
Circle and color 4 of each:

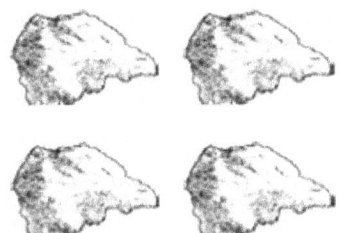

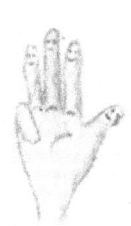

Write the number 4 using the arrows as a guide:

Four
Circle sets of 4 in each row:

- - - - - - - - - - - - - - -

- - - - - - - - - - - - - - -

Join each bee to its beehive:
(start at the black dot)

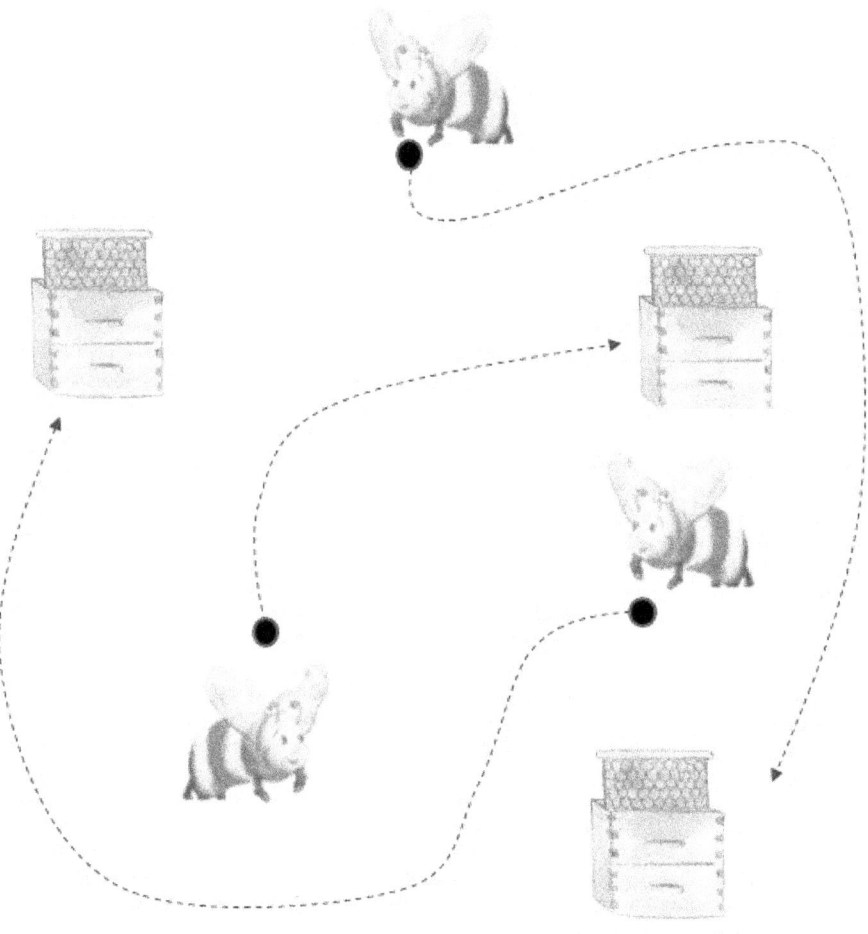

Ask your child to use his finger to trace over the line, before using a pencil.

Circle and color four bones for each dog:
(Color the bones different colors for each dog)

Question: Are there more dogs or more bones?
Question: How many bones are left over?

Matching

Color the matching one:

Recognizing Patterns

Color the dots according to the pattern, encouraging your child to name the colors.

Green, red, green, …

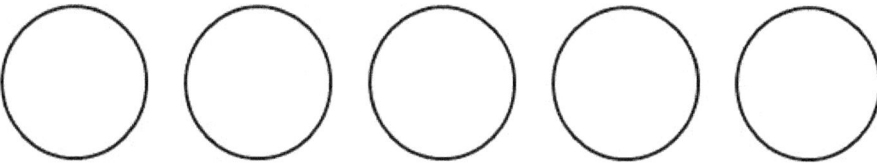

Blue, yellow, blue, …

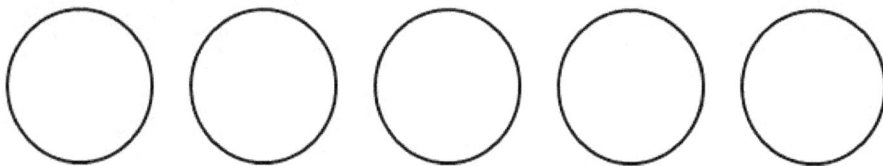

Yellow, orange, yellow, …

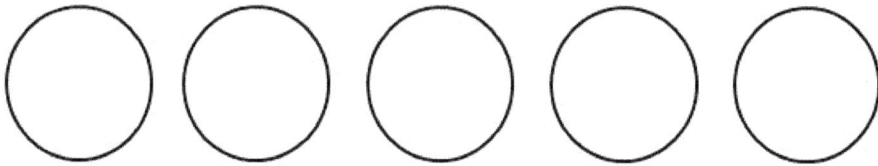

Write the number 4 using the arrows as a guide:

Tall & Short

Circle the shorter one in each set:

Small Medium Big

In each row, draw the missing one according to its size:

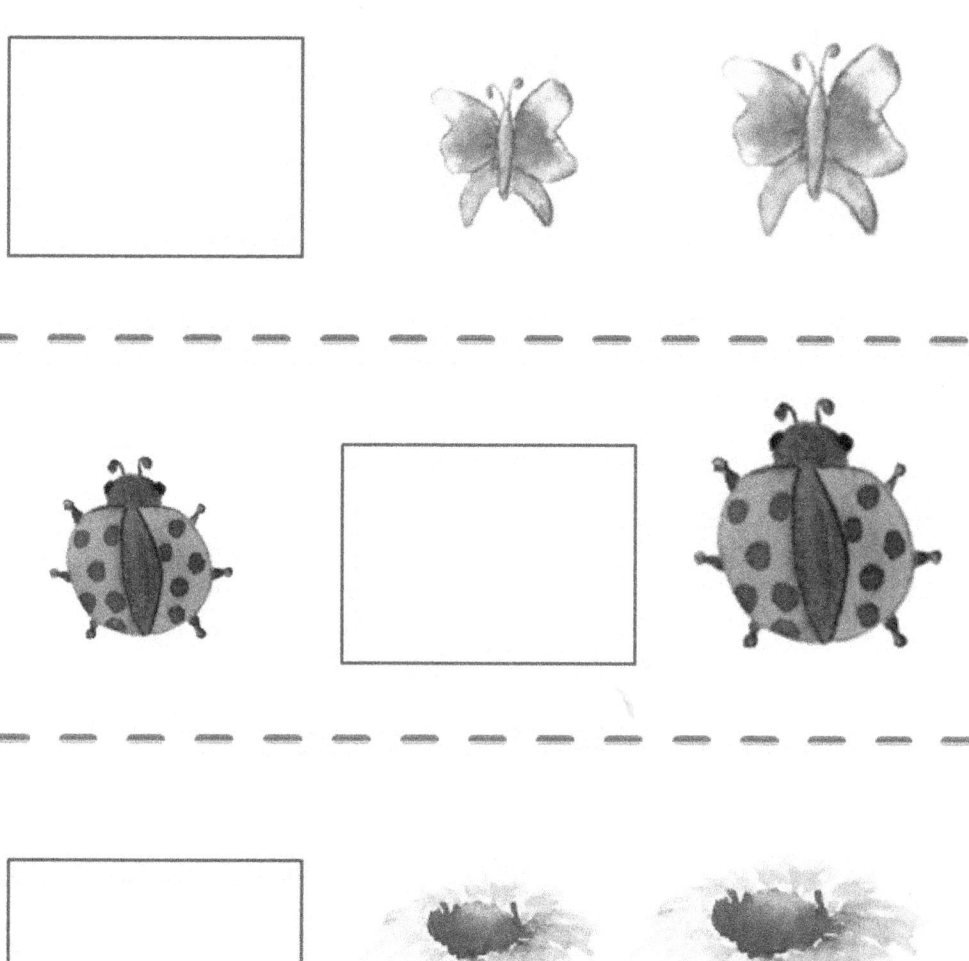

How Many?

In each row, count the animals and circle the correct number.

1 2 3

2 3 4

Write the number 4 using the arrows as a guide:

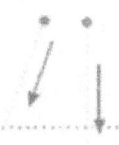 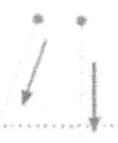 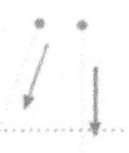 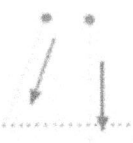

Color the set with the bigger amount in each row:

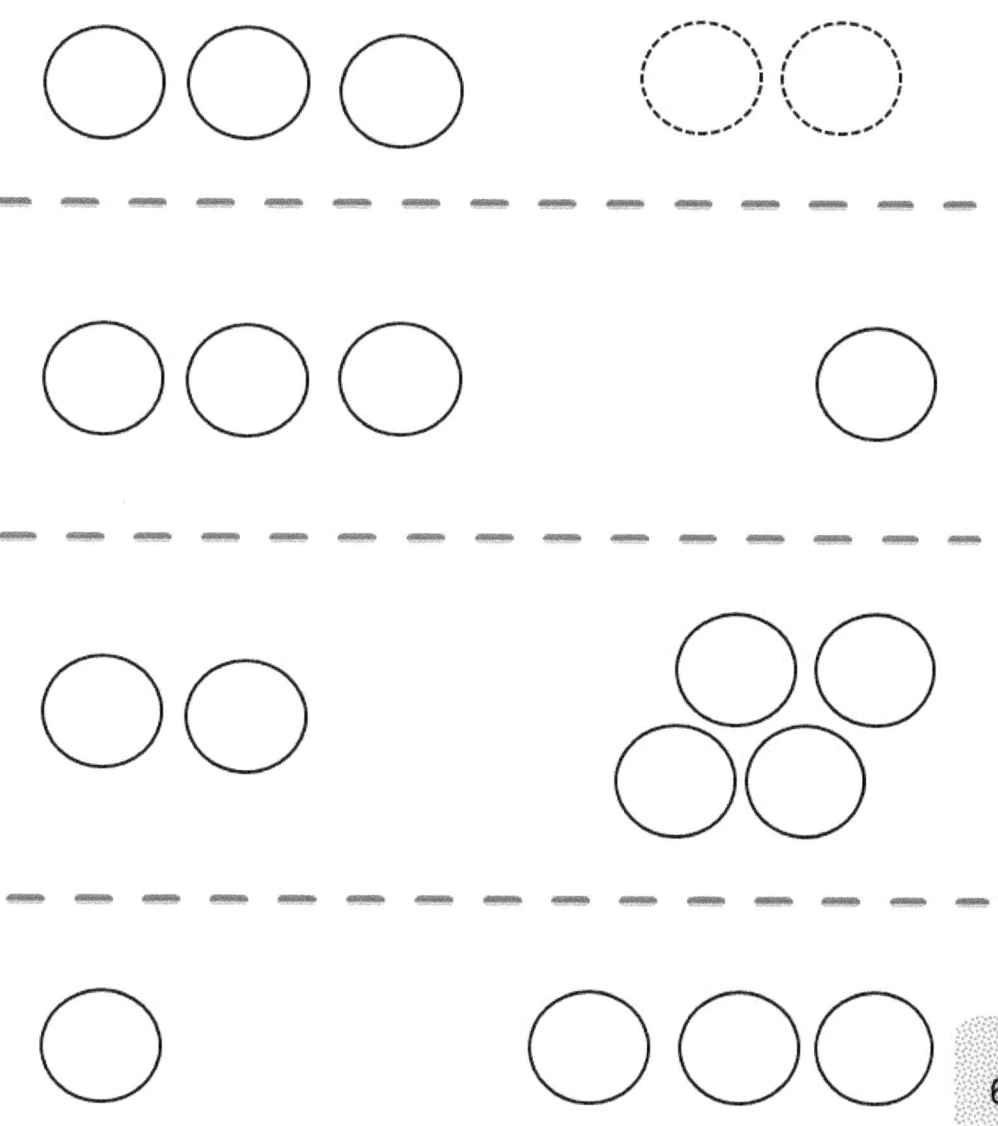

Follow the instructions:

Draw 3 carrots for each rabbit.

Draw 4 eggs for each chicken.

Draw 5 seeds for each turkey.

Matching numbers to quantities

Draw a line matching the number to its amount:

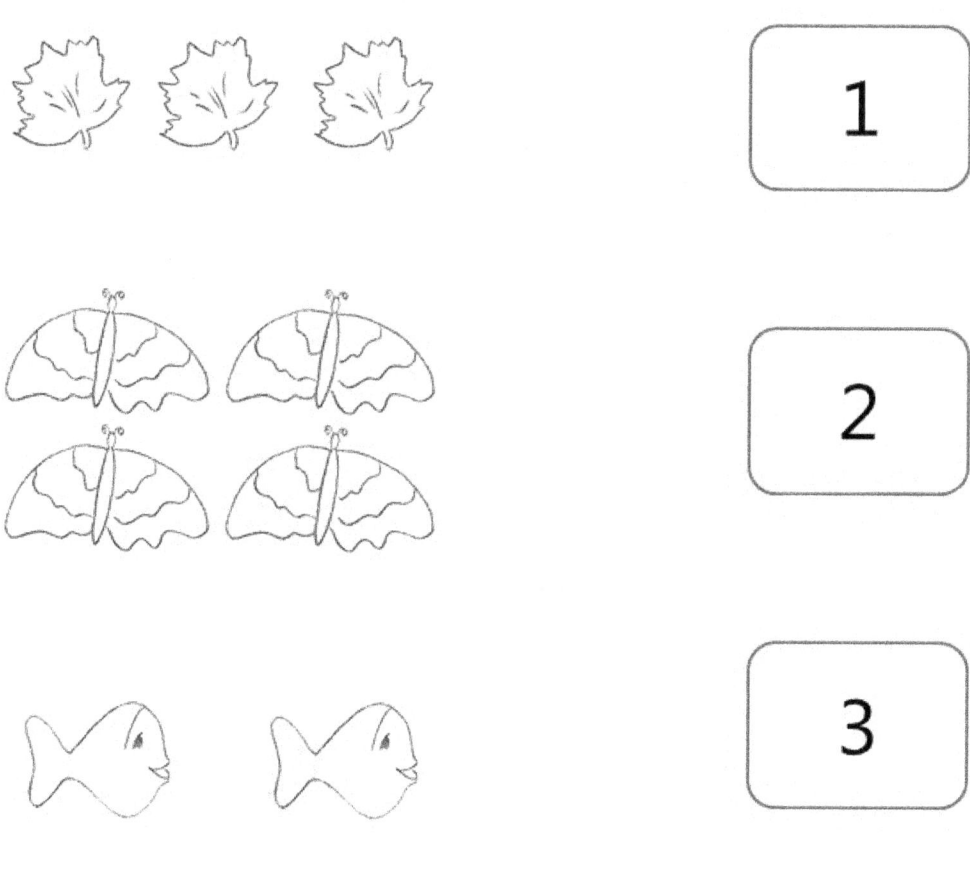

Let's draw circles:

Join the dots, starting at the black dot,
Using the arrows as a guide:

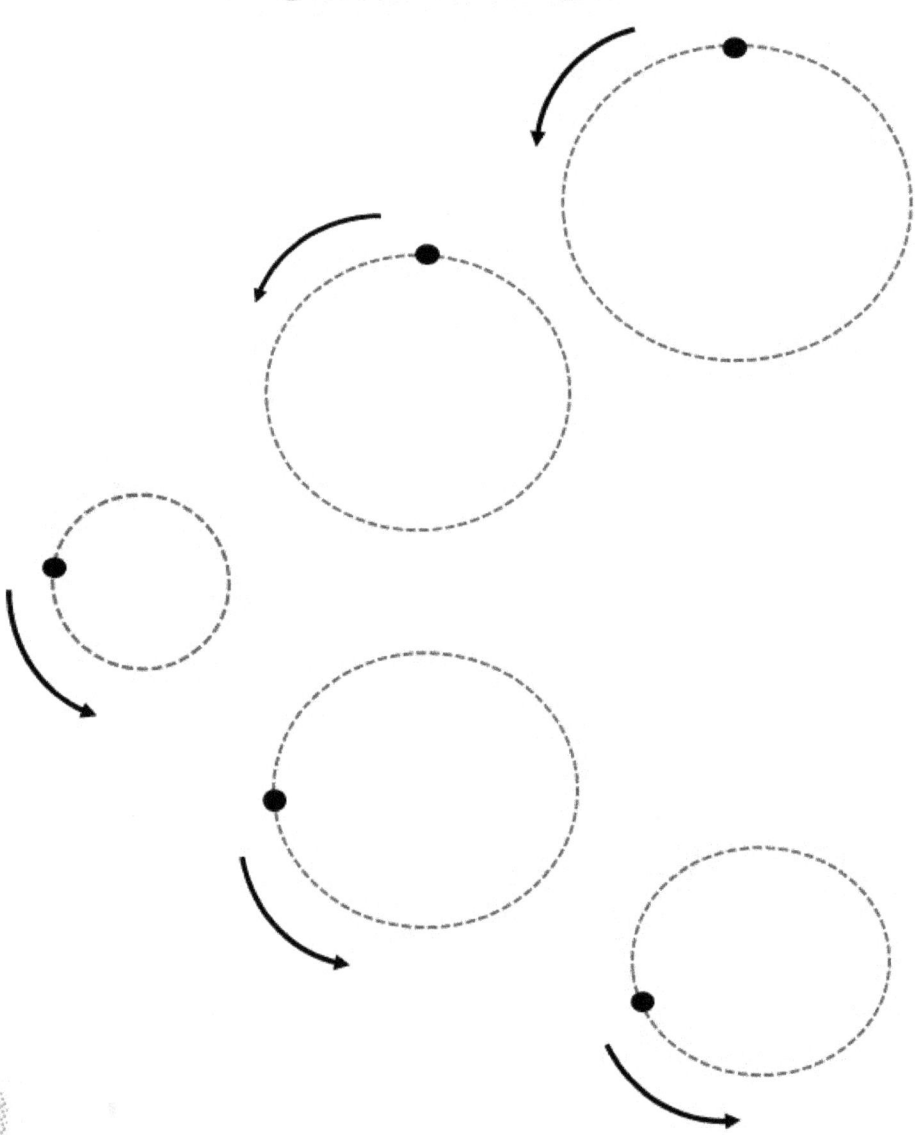

Color squares according to the number:

Follow the instructions:

Color: 5 fish yellow.
4 fish green.
3 fish blue.
2 fish purple.
1 fish red.

Complete:

Cut out and paste the matching cards, from the page at the end of the workbook.

Color the set with the smaller amount in each row:

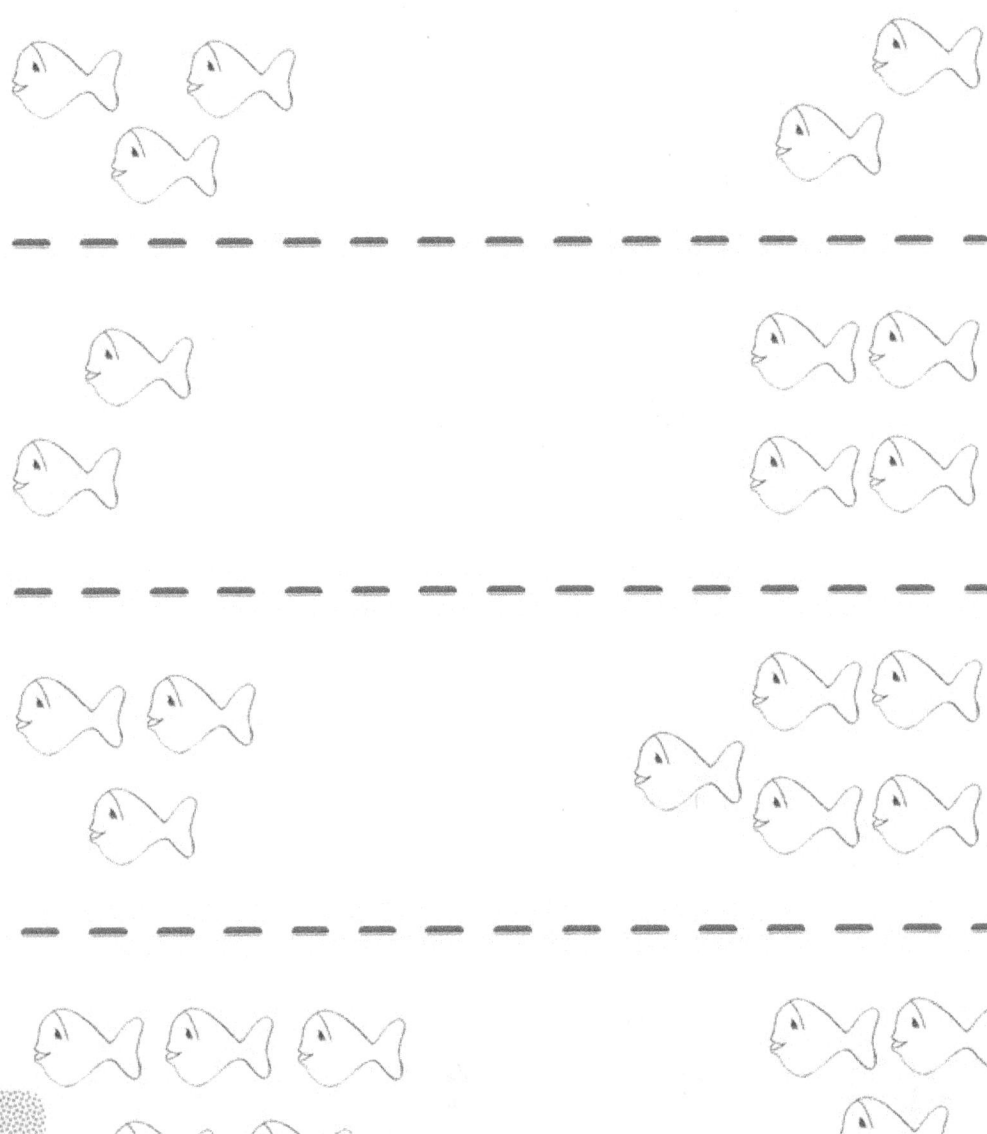

Follow the instructions:

Color the triangles red.

Color the squares orange.

Color the circles yellow.

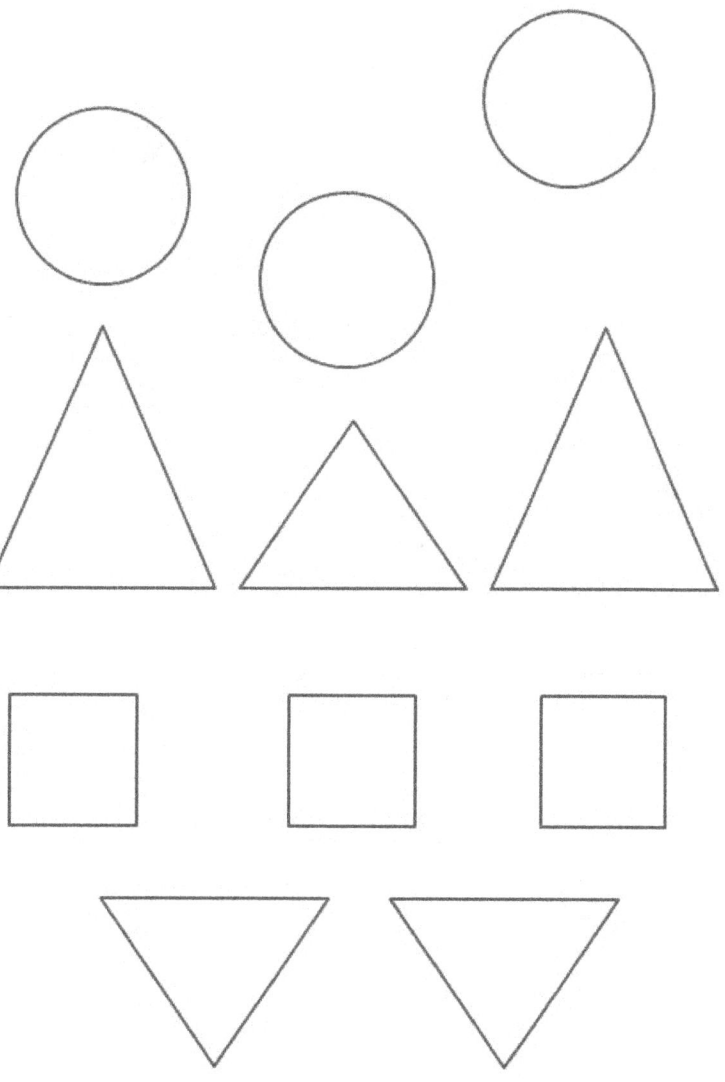

Five

Circle and color 5 of each:

Write the number 5 using the arrows as a guide:

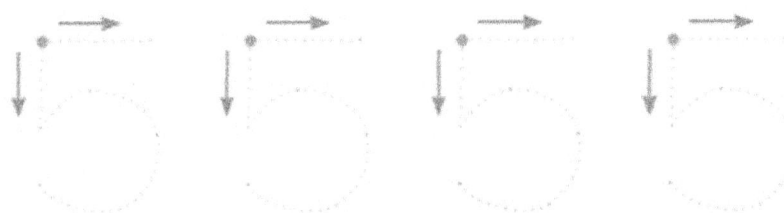

Five
Circle sets of five in each row:

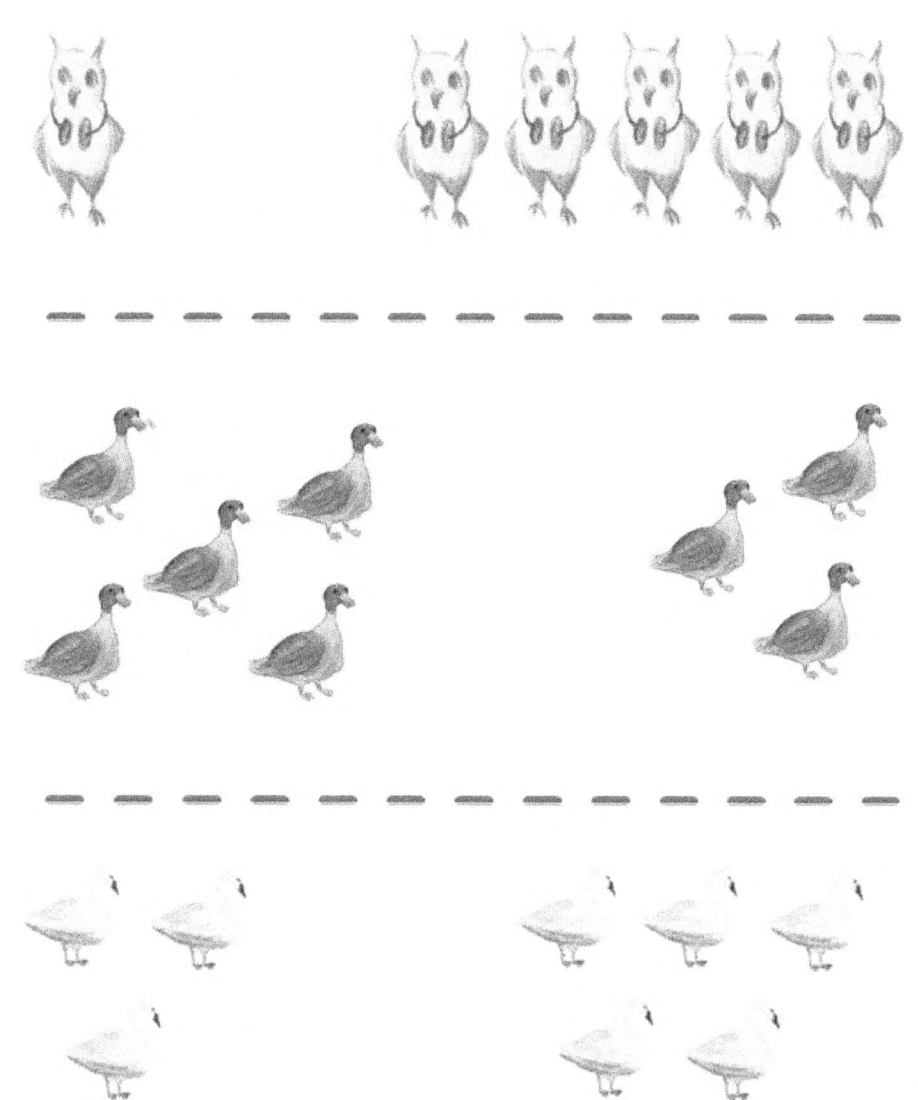

Join each parrot to its peanut:
(start at the black dot)

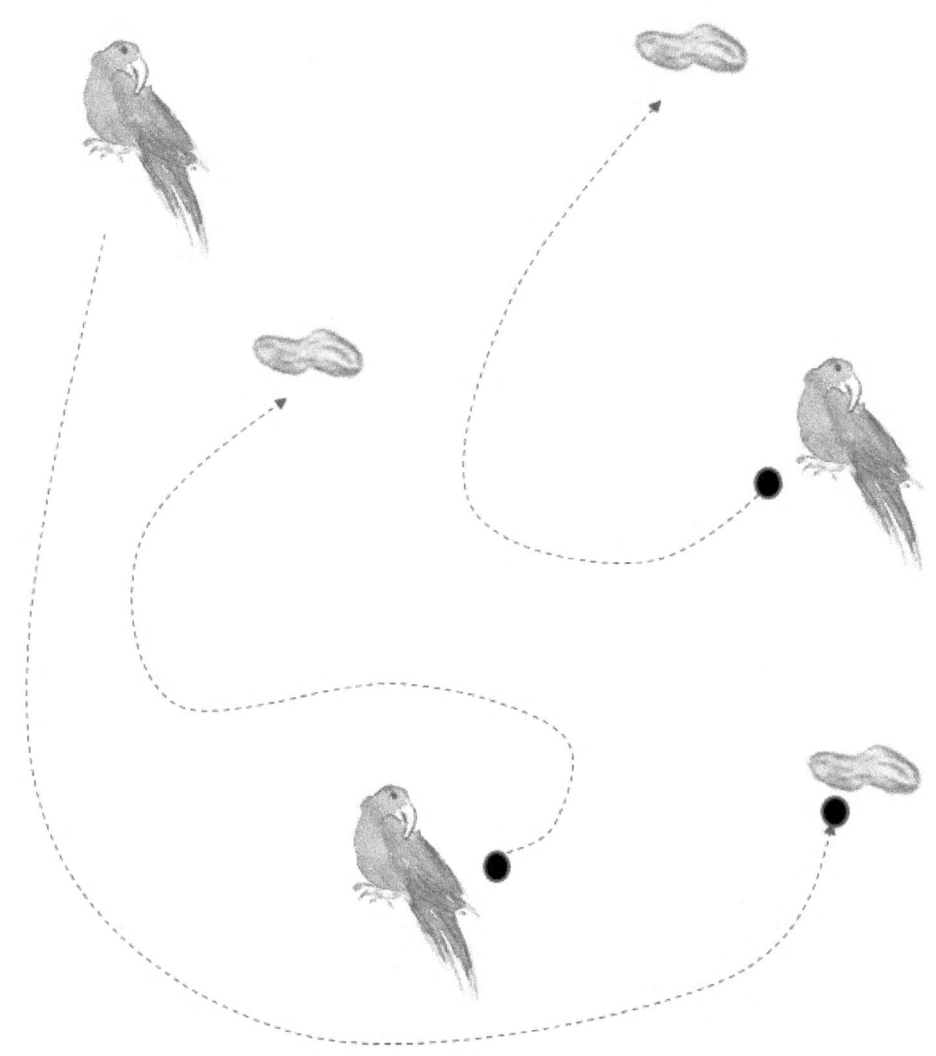

76

Ask your child to use his finger to trace over the line,
before using a pencil.

Make Sets
Circle and color 5 fish for each aquarium:
(Color the fish different colors for each aquarium)

Question: Are there more fish or more aquariums?
Question: how many fish are there without an aquarium?
Draw an aquarium for the fish left over.

Matching
Color the matching one:

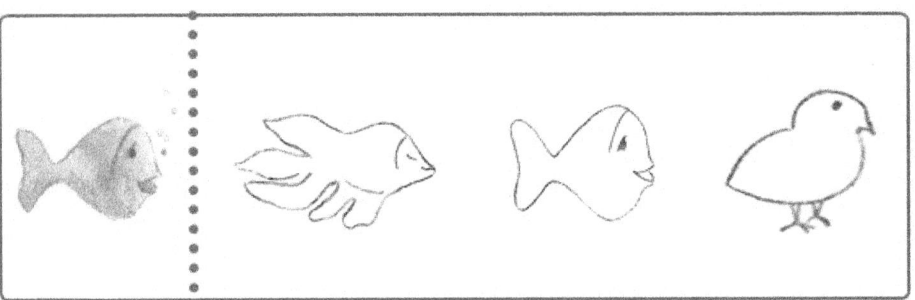

Recognizing Patterns

Color the dots according to the pattern,
encouraging your child to name the colors:

Yellow, blue, yellow …

Red, blue, red …

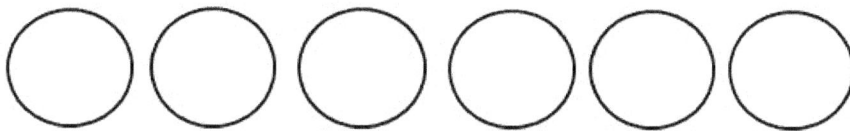

Green, pink, green …

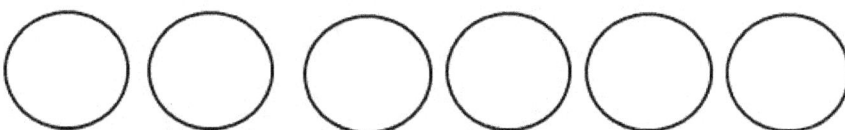

Write the number 5 using the arrows as a guide:

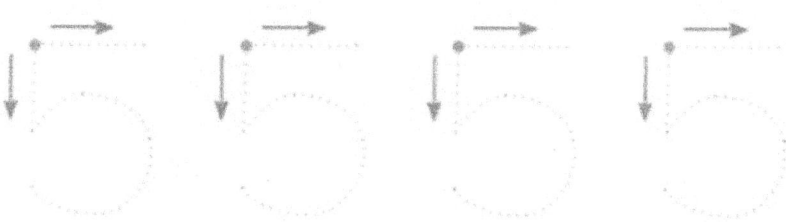

Tall & Short
Circle the shorter one in each set:

Small Medium Big

In each row, draw the missing one according to its size:

 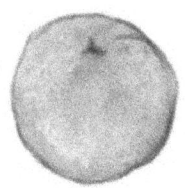 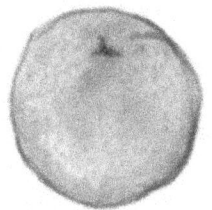

- - - - - - - - - - - - - - - -

- - - - - - - - - - - - - - - -

  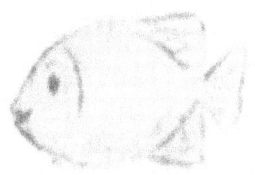

How Many?

Count the pandas in each row, and circle the correct number:

      3 4 5

     3 4 5

       3 4 5

Write the number 5 using the arrows as a guide:

 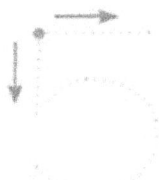 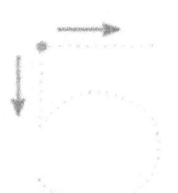 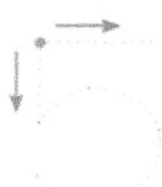

Color the set with the Bigger amount in each row:

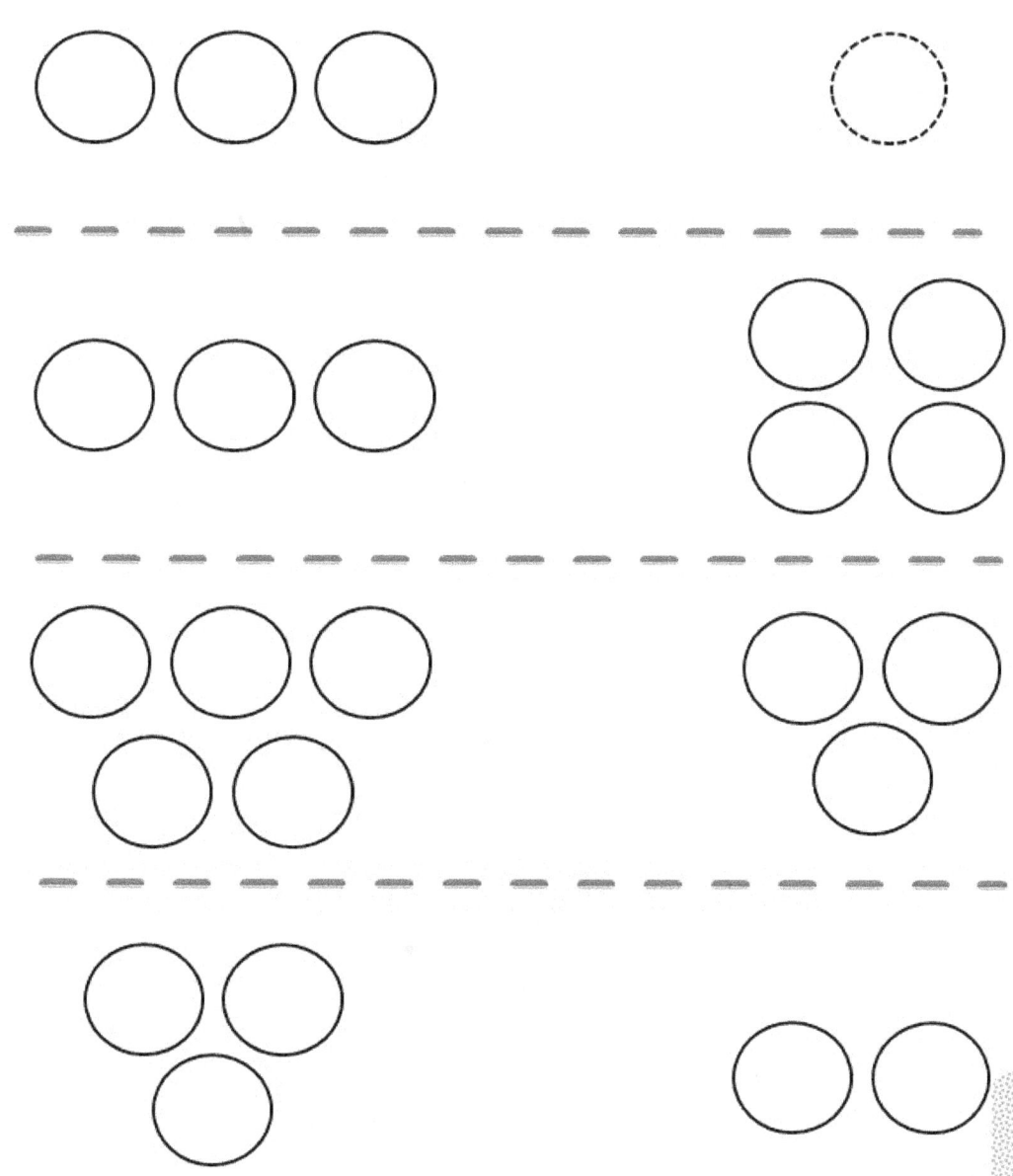

Odd One Out

Circle the odd one out in each row:

Write the number 5 using the arrows as a guide:

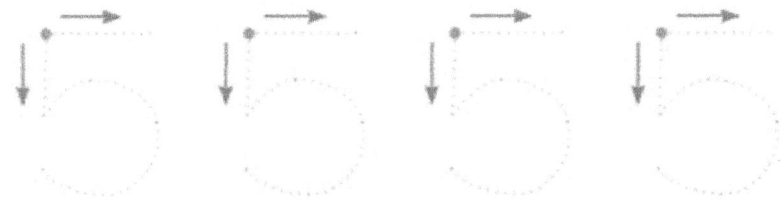

Marching Numbers To Quantities
Draw a line matching the
number to its amount:

Matching
Color the matching shapes:

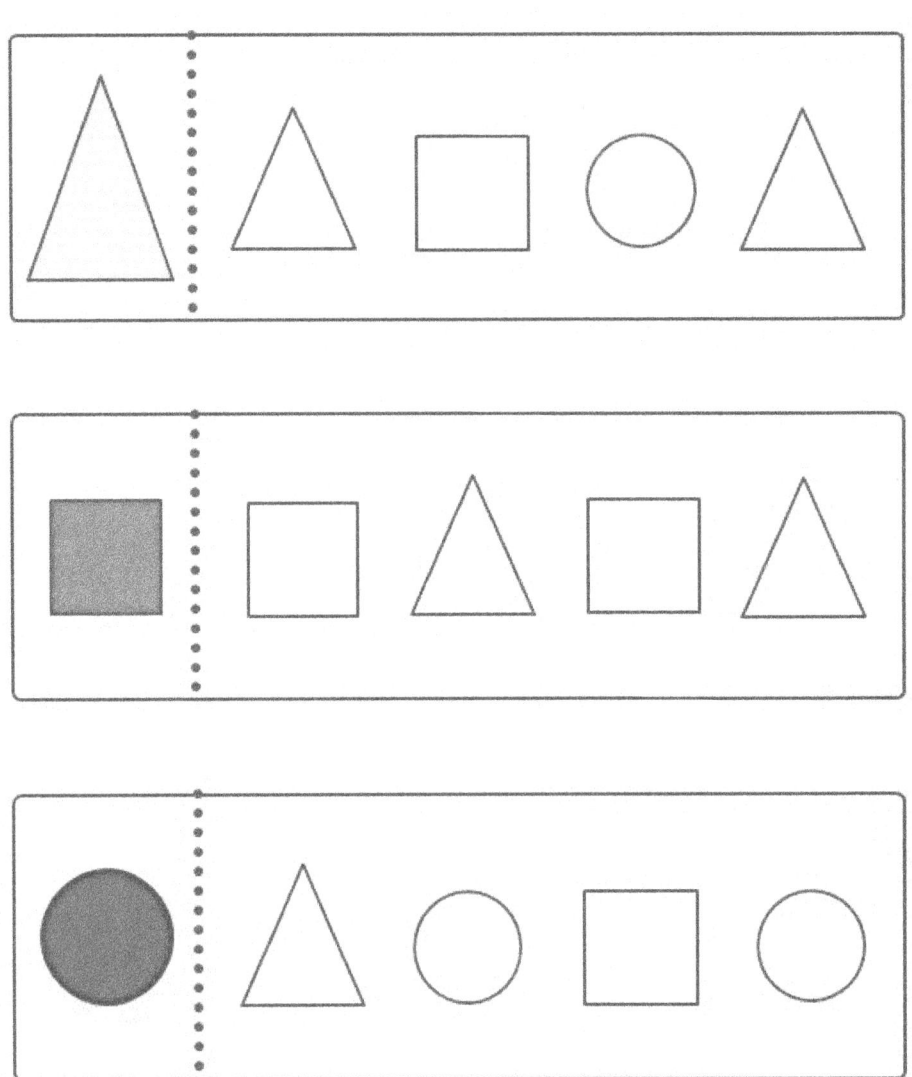

How Many Squares?

Color the squares in each column and write the amount.

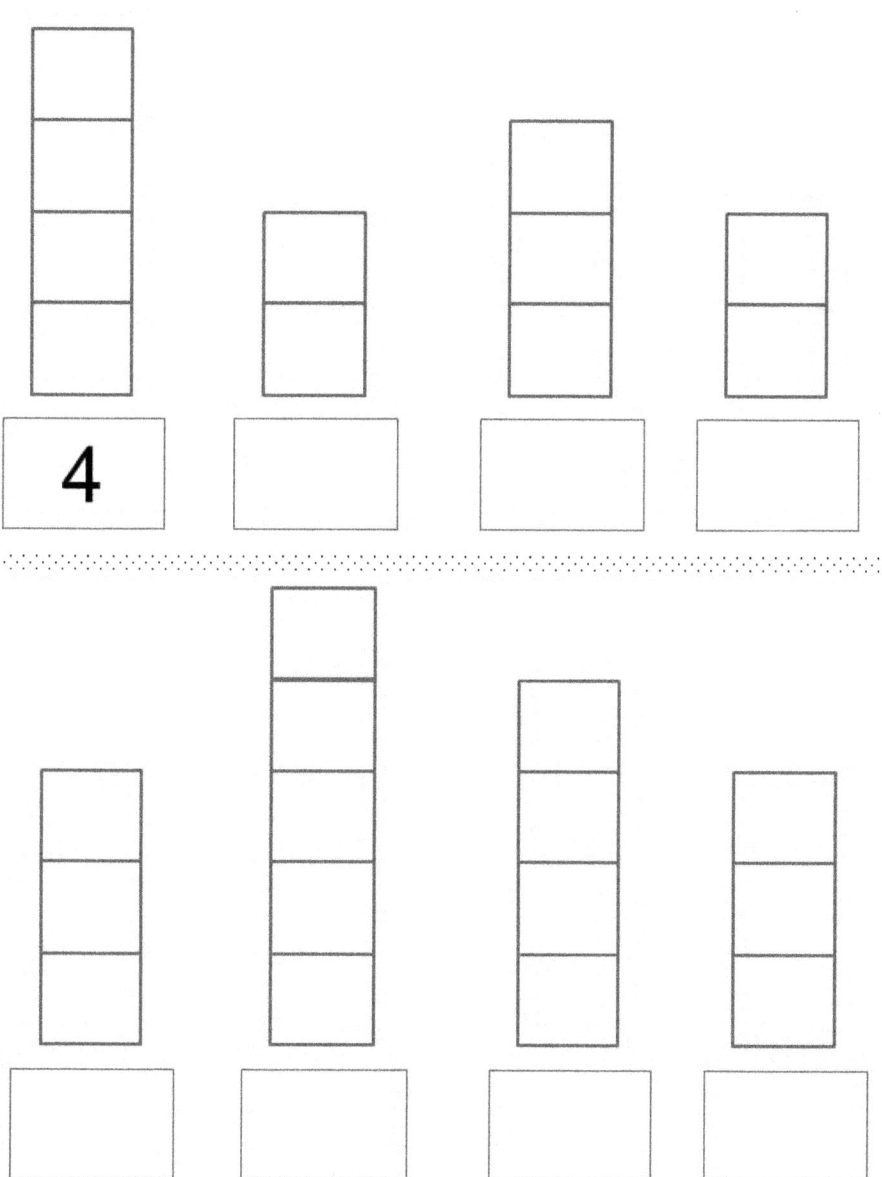

Matching
Match the number of fingers to the number of circles:

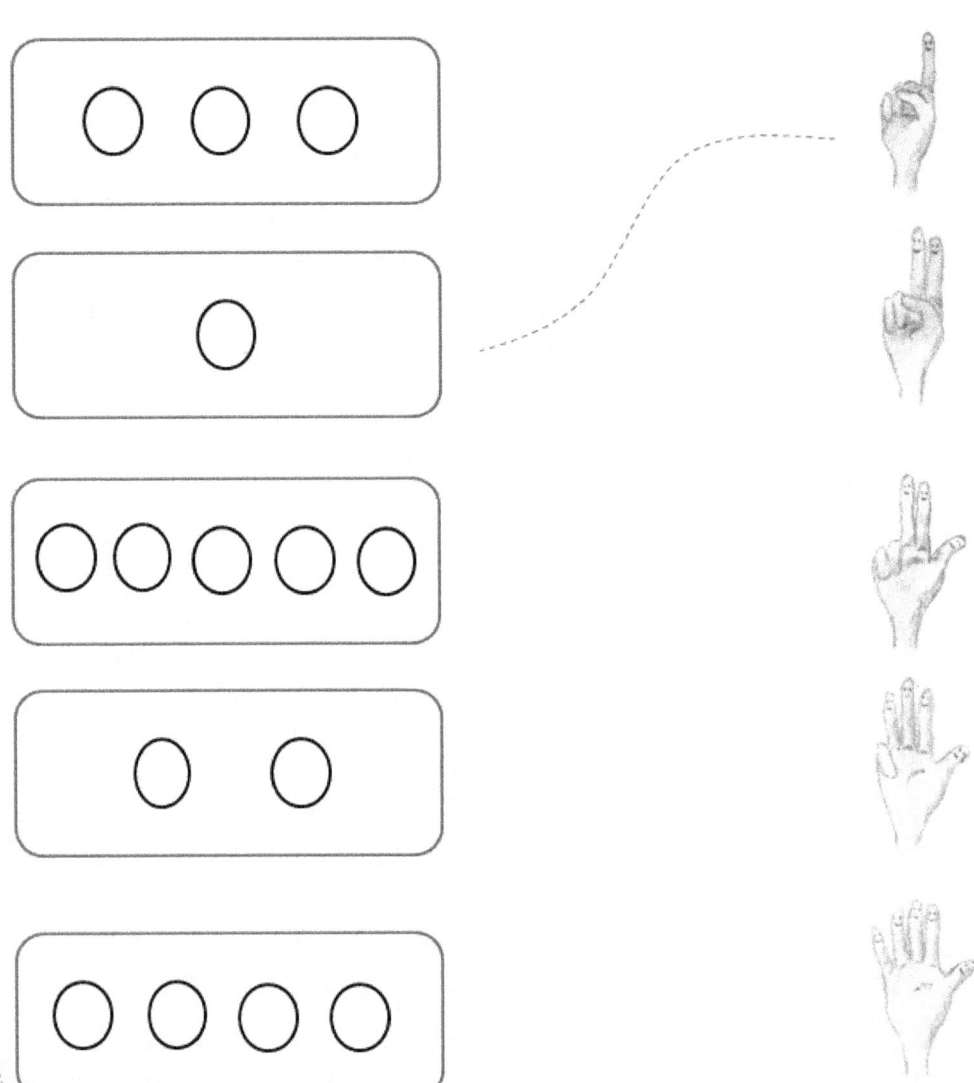

Color the set with the Smaller amount in each row:

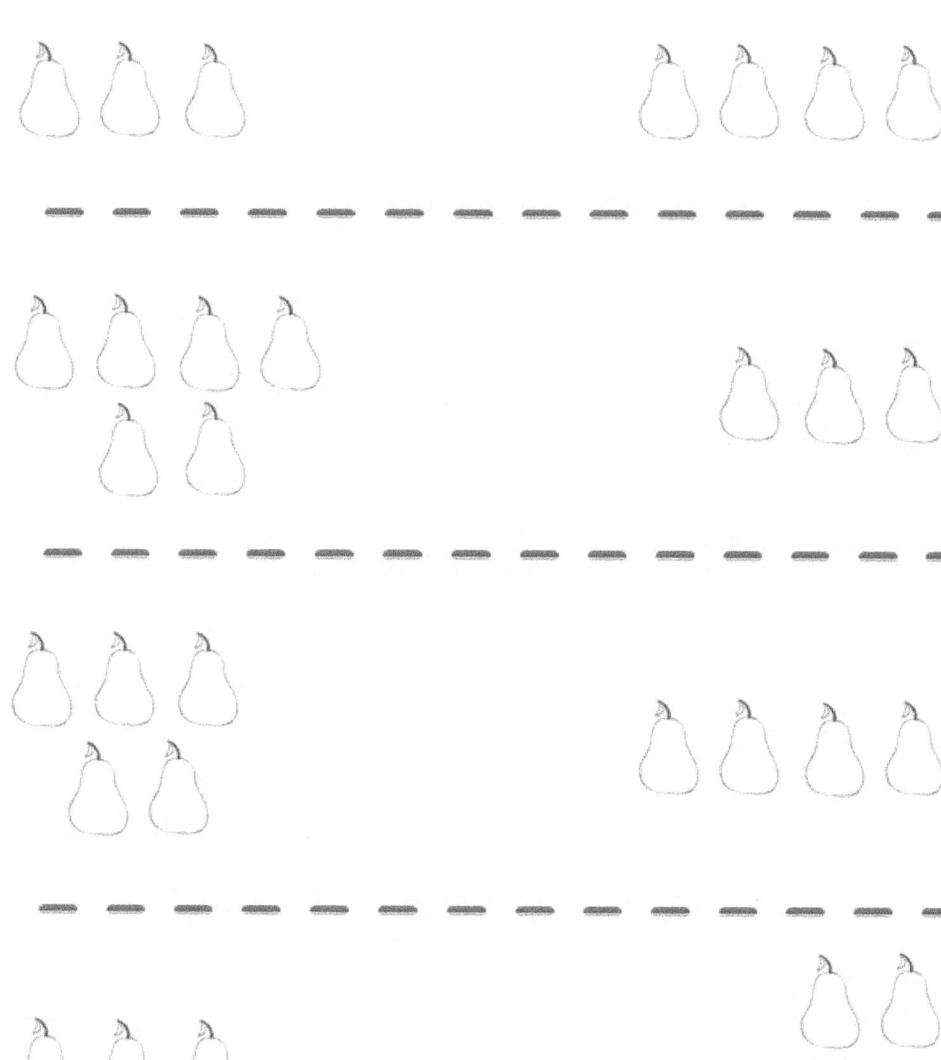

Fill in the missing shape:

Cut out and paste the matching cards, from the page at the end of the workbook.

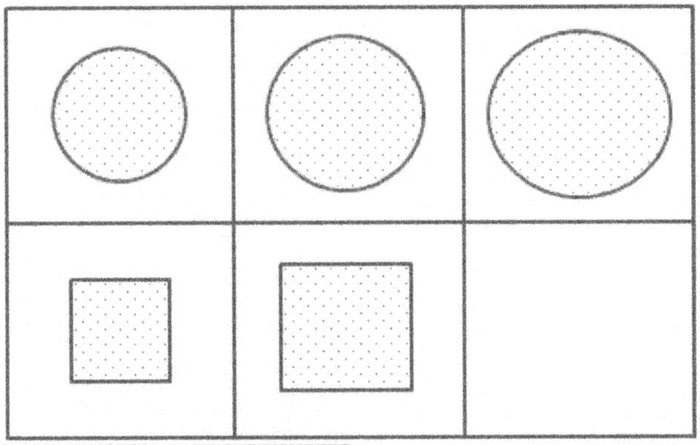

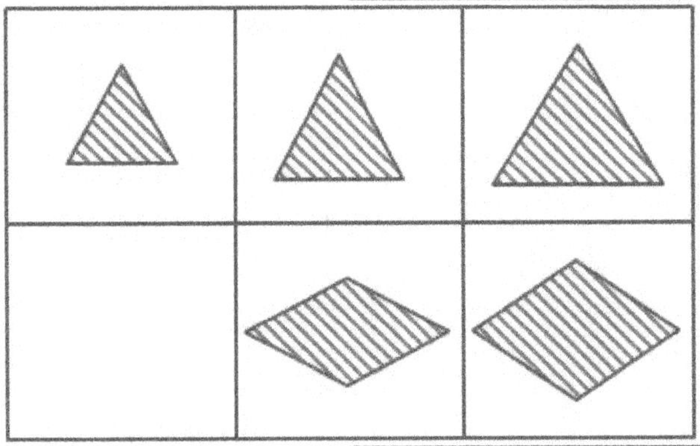

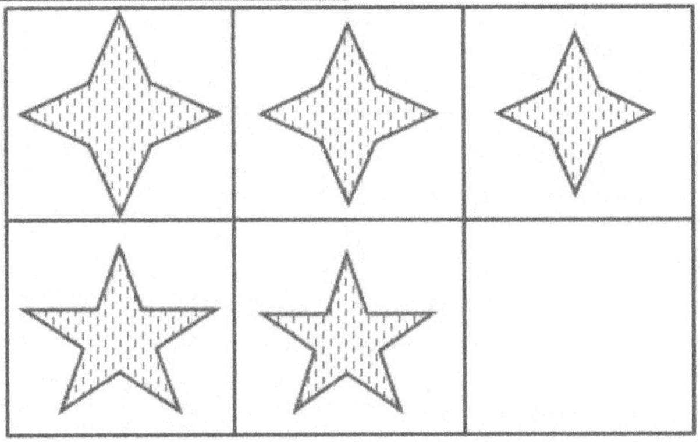

Follow the instructions:

Color:

1 square yellow.

2 squares green.

3 squares blue.

4 squares orange.

5 squares red.

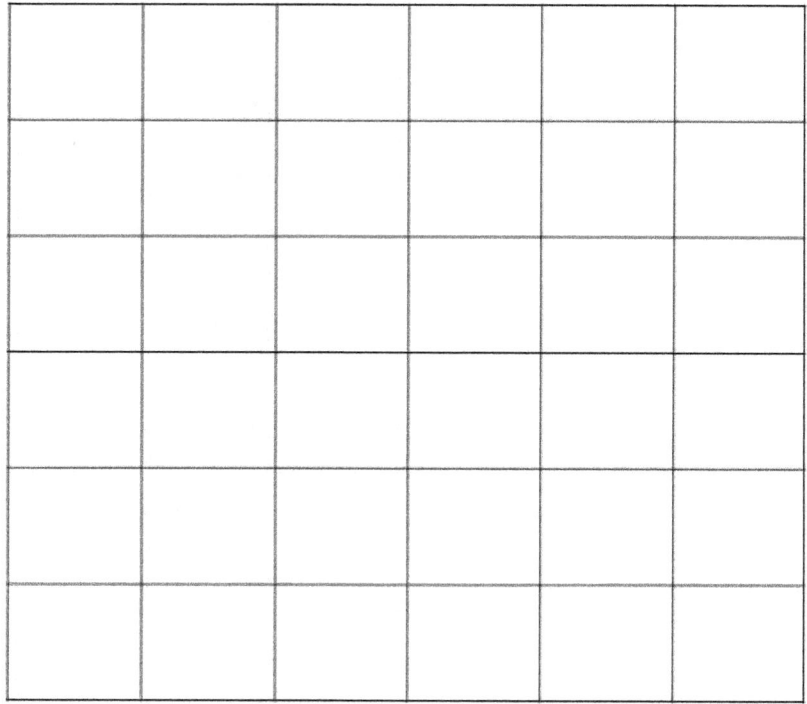

Cutting and pasting pages

Color each one and cut them out. Find their appropriate place and paste them in.

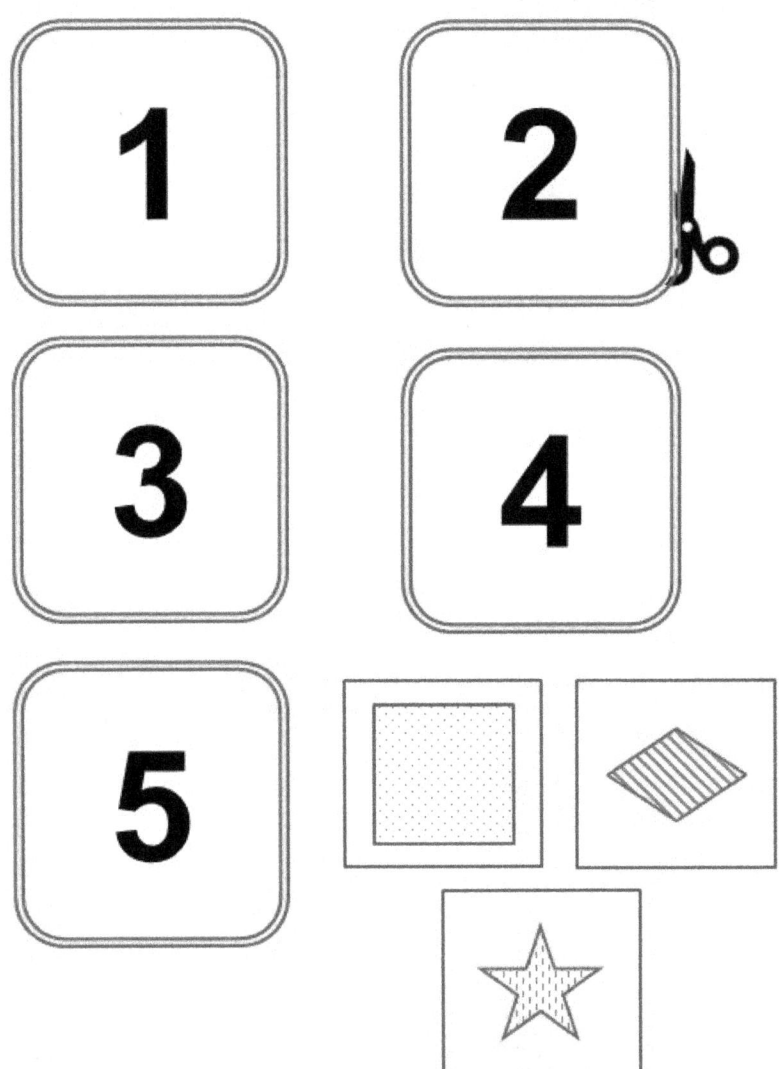

94

Color each one and cut them out. Find their appropriate place and paste them in:

Color the shapes and cut them out. Find their appropriate place and paste them in:

www.ingramcontent.com/pod-product-compliance
Lightning Source LLC
Chambersburg PA
CBHW081017040426
42444CB00014B/3247